The King's Bodyguard

A Martial Arts Legend Meets the King of Rock 'n Roll

By **Dave Hebler**

BearManor Media

Orlando, Florida

The King's Bodyguard: A Martial Arts Legend Meets the King of Rock 'n Roll
Copyright ©2022 Dave Hebler. All Rights Reserved.

No part of this book may be reproduced in any form or by any means, electronic, mechanical, digital, photocopying or recording, except for the inclusion in a review, without permission in writing from the publisher.

This book is an independent work of research and commentary and is not sponsored, authorized or endorsed by, or otherwise affiliated with, any motion picture studio or production company affiliated with the films discussed herein. All uses of the name, image, and likeness of any individuals, and all copyrights and trademarks referenced in this book, are for editorial purposes and are pursuant of the Fair Use Doctrine.

The views and opinions of individuals quoted in this book do not necessarily reflect those of the author.

The promotional photographs and publicity materials reproduced herein are in the author's private collection (unless noted otherwise). These images date from the original release of the films and were released to media outlets for publicity purposes.
Cover Illustration by Oisin McGillion Hughes.

Published in the USA by
BearManor Media
1317 Edgewater Dr. #110
Orlando, FL 32804
www.BearManorMedia.com

Softcover Edition
ISBN-10: 000
ISBN-13: 978-1-62933-879-8

Printed in the United States of America

Table of Contents

Foreword   vii

Preface   ix

Introduction   xi

Prologue   xv

How It All Began   xv

Chapter 1: The Beginning   1

Chapter 2: Elvis and Martial Arts   5

Chapter 3: My First Assignment – Lake Tahoe   17

Chapter 4: Fun with Elvis   23

Chapter 5: The Crazy Ladies   35

Chapter 6: Random Stories   41

    Image Section   49

Chapter 7: Playing with the Colonel   57

Chapter 8: Elvis and Gospel Music   61

Chapter 9: The Drugs and the Hit   71

Chapter 10: Getting Fired! Elvis What Happened?   77

Chapter 11: The Aftermath   85

Foreword

Ed Parker Jr.

My father, Ed Parker, Sr., brought Martial Arts to the Americas from the territory of Hawaii prior to its induction into statehood. My father was named "The Father of American Karate" by *Blackbelt Magazine,* as he created and pioneered his own style of Kenpo Karate in America.

Ed Parker, Sr. was noted as the main catalyst for launching the careers of Bruce Lee and Chuck Norris, as well as numerous other notable Martial Artists. Because of my father's teacher/student relationship with Dave Hebler, I have known Dave from my birth.

Dave Hebler became one of my father's most trusted and accomplished black belts in the 1960's. My father often used Dave for his Martial Arts demonstrations and promotions. Dave also managed a number of Ed Parker Karate franchised schools.

I recall hearing stories of Dave Hebler in the beginning stages of his Martial Arts career bouncing me on his knee. I often joke about him bouncing me on his knee again, just for old time's sake. I am 61 years old and nearly twice Dave's weight. Dave declined my offer, and we both chuckled about that.

My father met the legendary Elvis Presley in the early 1960s. Their first meeting developed into a deep and lasting friendship up to Elvis's passing in 1977.

My father not only was Elvis's friend and Martial Arts instructor, but was his confidant as well. Elvis often asked my father to provide personal security when he was available. I recall answering the phone often in the wee hours of the night as Elvis sought wisdom and advice from him.

One day my father told Elvis that his business' responsibilities demanded more attention. He needed to recommend one of his top black belts to fill the role as lead bodyguard and protector. Elvis's bodyguard needed a full-time job.

My father's first recommendation, out of hundreds of black belts in his system, was Mr. Dave Hebler. Elvis chose Dave Hebler, and Dave served in this capacity as bodyguard for Elvis for many years.

Dave has a wealth of historical knowledge that comes from being behind the curtains in the private life and history of Elvis Presley.

The pages of Elvis Presley's life contain missing knowledge that only Dave Hebler can provide. I recommend anyone in need of historical perspective on Elvis Presley to read this book. It will be a valuable asset to your library.

Preface

Robert Hammer

Dave Hebler followed the way of Bushido religiously. I sparred with all seven of the Memphis Mafia, as Elvis Presley's bodyguards liked to call themselves. Dave was the only one who could kick my ass. He had control, so he never hurt me. He was a 3rd or 5th-degree Black Belt at the time. I was a Brown Belt with skills. I learned a lot about how to be a real, professional bodyguard from Dave. By the numbers, a protective service doesn't mean you get into fights. If you're good, there is only calm. No troubles, no threats. All quiet around the client. That was Dave's style.

On a rare occasion, he would apply a simple wrist lock. Everything ended quickly without notice. Dave was always modest and humble. Oh, and he was a great driver. One time a huge Lincoln Continental headed straight for us on the freeway in Memphis. Dave, behind the wheel, had his usual poker face on as he casually crossed over three lanes of oncoming traffic and went up a highway off-ramp, avoiding any accident with this drunken, crazed driver. Everyone screamed and thought they were about to die. Dave didn't say a word or change his expression. After we all calmed down, Dave said, "Yeah, that's the way they drive in Memphis." That was vintage Dave Hebler.

On one of the few times Elvis flew a commercial airline, we encountered a real, huge drunk. He sighted Elvis and was determined to fight him. Profanity and insults were hurled. We just ignored him, but he wouldn't stop. Elvis was no pussycat. He had lots of guys to spar with and a bit of a temper. Dave could see that E. was going to smack this guy. Problem is it inevitably ends up becoming a lawsuit for E. And so, Dave gets up and slowly walks over to the guy and gives him a triple-back-fist combination to his jaw. The drunk went to sleep and stayed that way for the entire trip. We got off the flight from Vegas to Memphis with everybody safe and sound. Dave never said a word.

Those are the fondest memories I have of Dave Hebler.

Introduction

Chuck Sullivan

When Dave Hebler began his Karate career in 1959, the art, even the word Karate, was virtually unknown in the United States. It wasn't until a man from Hawaii named Edmund K. Parker finished his education at Brigham Young University in Utah and moved to Pasadena, California, where he opened the first Kenpo Karate School in the United States and created the headquarters for what has become a worldwide network of students and instructors.

At that time, Ed Parker was the only person to hold the title of Black Belt in Kenpo in the United States (Hawaii was not yet a state). Dave and I became the fourth and fifth black belts in that lineage in what now numbers in the thousands.

Neither Dave nor I were youngsters at the time of our introduction to Kenpo. We had both been in the military. We were both married with young families, so there was a natural bond between the two of us; whereas, most of our fellow students were much younger with less life experience.

I happened to be in the class just above Dave, and we rarely were together on the mats for the first three years. It was after an incident where the members of the entire advanced class were lured away from the school, in an underhanded series of maneuvers by an extremely unscrupulous person. I was the lone exception from that group. I stayed with Ed Parker and therefore became the substitute instructor whenever Mr. Parker was unavailable to teach what had been the Intermediate Class, of which Dave was a member.

That class immediately became the new Advanced Class. It was then that I really got to know Dave. He was one of the more serious practitioners and, whenever I wanted to test anyone's freestyle fighting skills, I would match them against Dave. He was intense, but with excellent control. When Mr. Parker was available to teach, I then became a student alongside Dave and the others. That's when Mr. Parker would frequently match the two of us; it was always an awesome event.

Having studied with the person who was responsible for luring the advanced class away, I was privy to what he was teaching in Mr. Parker's absence. It was another style of Kung Fu that I was initially intrigued with, but came to have my doubts about, which contributed in part to my staying with Ed Parker and his system of Kenpo. One night, I remember thinking that I'd try some of those moves while freestyling with Dave. Those moves were very powerful and would have been extremely effective had I been able to catch Dave, but even though he was unfamiliar with the moves or theory behind them, he had the good sense to stay just out of range. When I had run out of attack moves, he simply planted a fist right between my eyes with control. I felt the air compress against my face, but he never touched me. That's pinpoint accuracy.

Both Dave and I have been exposed to every style and system of Karate, and the masters who teach them, and have had ample opportunity to participate with any, or all of them, but neither of us ever had any inclination to jump ship into another style or system.

I'll never forget the night we were introduced to the infamous Bruce Lee, who at the time was a complete unknown. Ed Parker was very tight with the entertainment community at the time, privately teaching several high-powered stars, directors, and producers in Hollywood. Bruce had come to Southern California for the express purpose of breaking into the Biz. Ed Parker literally took him under his wing and introduced him around the Hollywood community.

Mr. Parker was scheduled to teach the regular Advanced Class one evening, and he had invited Bruce to observe. When the class had ended and we had changed into our street clothes, we were walking from the dressing room across the mats, shoes in hand, when Ed, still in his Gi, and another man, approached us halfway across the mats. He stopped us to introduce this young man, he said, "I want you guys to meet a hot, young Martial Artist; this is Bruce Lee." The group consisted of Dave, Danny Inasanto, and I think one other person, plus myself.

Introduction

Just as soon as Ed made the introduction he was called away, probably to the phone, so we were left alone with this young Chinese guy, who immediately took over the conversation by telling us that he had just returned from Hong Kong, which at the time was considered the mecca of Kung Fu. Our ears immediately perked up. This guy could be a wealth of information for us Westerners, so someone asked him what the Martial Arts were like in Hong Kong. His answer stunned us, when he said, "Ninety-five percent of what they're teaching in Hong Kong is commercial bullshit." Wow! That surely wasn't what we were expecting. Then one of us asked, "What's the other five percent like?" His answer again threw us for a loop. "Half of them are really trying, but they don't know what they're doing." Again, this was another unexpected jolt. The inevitable question arose, "What about those other guys, that last two-and-a-half percent?"

He said, with that sly sideways glance, "Oh, those guys are the real deal. But you 'round-eyes' couldn't get halfway down the alley alive where they work out. It's not a school; it's more of a secret society." We got the implication.

Then the young Mr. Lee dropped a real bomb, "I saw what you guys were doing earlier." This would have been during his observation of the class. He demonstrated what he had seen so perfectly you would have thought he was a member of that class since its inception. When he saw the confused expressions on our faces, and we didn't really reply, he knew he had us. He knew that we were doing what we were doing because Ed Parker was teaching it to us. So, he continued. "I was just wondering . . . *(long beat)* . . . because it was wrong!" He emphasized "WRONG."

I distinctly remember looking at Dave, and he seemed to grow three inches in height, while his chest expanded. When he nodded his head slightly in Bruce's direction, I got the message that he was asking, "Do you want him, or should I take him?" Bruce had just insulted the hell out of our instructor. Neither of us had ever heard anything like it before. With a look, I tried to convey that I'd like to hear what he had to say. He had a lot to say, and behold, he was right! The elements he was talking about did indeed violate a principle and would be better off out of the system. Unfortunately, it was also something of a traditional nature that was essential to a form or Kata, and was still being performed as such. It's sad to say, but most other, if not all other, styles or systems suffer from the same malady. When Bruce saw it, he couldn't resist expounding upon it.

Our meeting ended amicably, and Dave and I remained friendly, although not close with Bruce, until his death.

Insofar as David's trueness to the Art and its customs and courtesies, I recall the time when Dave had been promoted to a degree higher than I held at the time. This was no doubt due his relationship and employment by Elvis Presley and the fact that Dave was Elvis' in-house instructor. Elvis was always on a fast track for promotion by Ed Parker, who was the acknowledged head of the system, and naturally, Elvis' main mentor as well. So, when Elvis was promoted, it was necessary to keep Dave at least one degree above him. That's how it was that Dave was promoted ahead of me in rank at that point.

During that period, we all happened to be attending a class and promotion ceremony at the Pasadena Studio, the flagship school of the system. The protocol for the student body, of which Dave and I were senior members, was for the highest-ranked person to take the first position to the right of the class, and those below his rank, or in some cases, because of similar rank. Seniority would come into play and the most senior person would be to the others' right.

Normally, being the highest ranked person in attendance, the furthest right-hand position would have been mine. However, on that night Dave was also in attendance, so when I saw the rank on his belt, I realized that he was now the highest ranked belt in attendance, so I positioned myself to his left. I remember him looking at me and saying, "what're ya doing'?" to which I replied, "You're the highest rank here, this is where I belong." At which time, he grabbed my Gi jacket not too gently and yanked me to the other side of him. "You're my senior, and you'll always be my senior." I knew better than to argue.

Dave is Dave, and when the "Old Man" looked the class over, prior to the period of meditation, our positioning did not go unnoticed by him, but he never said a word, so all was well in Kenpo-land.

Prologue
How It All Began

Dave Hebler

This book is about my life with Elvis. It also goes into my life as a martial artist and how they tie together. I have included stories of the great times I had with Elvis, also some of the challenging times. You will read of my entire journey with Elvis: How I met him; how I became his bodyguard and martial arts instructor; my first assignment with him where I saw him perform live for the first time; some of the crazy things that happened while on the road, funny stories, my thoughts about the book *Elvis: What Happened?*, and why and how I was a part of it, when I was fired, and the aftermath when Elvis passed.

I grew up in Pittsfield, MA, the oldest of five children. Pittsfield is in the western part of the state of Massachusetts in an area called the Berkshire Hills, a beautiful area well known for its fall foliage and beautiful scenery.

Not so beautiful was the tenement apartment where I lived with my four brothers and my parents. Our apartment was one of six in a tenement building built around 1900 and, as we like to joke, condemned in 1901. Our apartment consisted of a kitchen, living room, 2 1/2 bedrooms, and one bathroom. My poor mother had to put up with it all. I shared a bed with my brother Paul. Don and Dennis shared another bed, and Doug had a crib.

We didn't have a phone or television. We also didn't have a vehicle or hot water. During the winter we had to stuff rags under the windows and doors to keep the snow from coming in. Our stove was old and broken down. Anything that needed to be heated had to be heated by that stove like hot water for baths and cooking.

We also had the dreaded cellar that was for all six apartments, which was a really scary place. With cinder floors and a low ceiling, each apartment had its own compartment that contained a large barrel where the fuel oil was stored. My job was to trudge down to our compartment with a 5-gallon can and a flashlight, fill the can, and haul it back up to the second floor where our apartment was located. It was an exciting time in the winter; I couldn't wait for my brother Don to get old enough to take over that chore. It was a terrifying experience being down there: no lights, and my imagination running wild—surely monsters lived down there, didn't they?

If we wanted to play, we invented the game. If we wanted to go somewhere, we walked or hitch-hiked.

We had rats and cockroaches in abundance. I was 16 years old when I realized there were actually houses that didn't have those warm creatures. You haven't lived until you have had the experience of having a rat or a cockroach run across your face while you are sleeping!

When I came across one of those little rascals, I endeavored to sharpen my hunting skills. I stationed myself across the room from a rat hole with my trusty BB gun and waited for a rat to come out. I became a sharpshooter shooting rats. The NRA would be so proud of me.

I also hunted cockroaches with a rubber-band gun that I manufactured. It was a square dowel, about 12 inches long, with an attached square dowel grip. Attached to the grip were three spring-loaded clothespins. From our butcher I got heavy-duty rubber bands that I stretched from the front of my "gun" to the clothespins. Now armed with the latest in cockroach armament, I turned off the lights in the room, waited a few minutes, then turned the lights back on and shot those cockroaches stupid enough to venture out.

Our apartment was a rowdy place, although I never thought of it that way. It was just the place where we lived. Even though we were desperately poor, we were quite happy. We always had food to eat and clothes on our backs. All in all, despite being deprived of material things, we were content because of our parents, especially our mother. She did everything in her power to provide for her children. Our parents loved us unconditionally and did everything they could

Prologue

with the little they had to take care of us. My brothers and I are living proof that love conquers all.

Being poor, if you wanted something and that something cost money, you had to somehow earn that money. So, my very first job was as a caddie at a local country club. I was 8 years old and carried bags that were bigger than me for 18 holes. I earned a whopping sum of $1.35 per round of golf, about $0.30 an hour.

A few years later, I really wanted a fishing pole and reel. It cost $14.00. I got a job at a bowling alley about three miles from our apartment. At 6:00 in the evening I arrived at the bowling alley and went to work manually setting pins on two side-by-side alleys. It was kind of an exciting job dodging all the flying pins coming my way at high velocity. I made $0.07 per string for my efforts. Months later I earned the $14.00 to pay for that rod and reel.

When I was 13, as I said, I owned a BB gun, and so did my friends. One day we all went out into the woods to play and had a little war shooting at each other. I lost that war because the last thing my right eye saw was that little bit of copper flash just before it struck my eye and took its vision away forever. I don't remember the pain, but as my friends walked me home the words, *I'm blind, I'm blind,* kept screaming through my mind. The horror of that statement became true, I was blind . . . forever . . . in my right eye.

Like most people, I have had numerous hurdles in my life. The biggest, however, has been the fact I have no depth perception because I remain blind in one eye. This horrible episode was most significant because of the way it negatively affected everything that came later in my life. I am telling this story for you to understand what a huge deal this was.

The next huge hurdle happened when I was 17, a senior in high school. The course I studied was called "technical." It was mostly taught by engineers from the very large General Electric Company in my hometown. This course concentrated on science in various areas, such as math, physics, *et cetera*. At the time, General Electric had a terrific apprentice toolmaker and apprentice draftsman program available to the children of General Electric employees who could qualify for the program. During my senior year of high school, my dad, who worked for General Electric, had me apply for the program. I passed all the requirements and was approved for the program upon graduation. It was a four-year program that consisted of college courses combined with on-the-job training. It was one week of college alternating with one week of work for four years. At the end of the four years, I'd have a BS degree and a Journeyman Toolmaker certificate. I'd also get a job at the General Electric *and* a weekly paycheck during those four years of college and on-the-job training.

WOW! I was excited, but then my acceptance in the program was cancelled! The reason for the cancellation: because I was blind in one eye, they were afraid that something might happen to my good eye during the OJT part of the program. I appealed their decision as hard as I could. I even offered to wear safety glasses, but I was just a 17 year old kid with no influence or power. Was I devastated? You bet I was. I was also angry. Knowing that my future lay elsewhere, I joined the Air Force in November of 1955, and ended up at March Air Force Base outside Riverside, CA. I spent almost four years there as a Senior Intelligence Operations Specialist. My daughters find it endlessly amusing to put the words "intelligence" and "Dad" in the same sentence.

My duties included photographic interpretation and navigational chart plotting, accumulation and evaluation of intelligence data for reports and briefings, and the responsibility for maintaining up-to-date target information. In 1958, I started martial arts training in Kenpo karate. My involvement in the martial arts remains to this day, some 62 years later.

There were several Hawaiian guys in my squadron who were training in Kenpo, and they allowed me to train with them. The following year, in 1959, I planned to enroll at Pasadena City College in Pasadena, CA. I had to enlist by June 1, 1959 to get an early-out honorable discharge from the Air Force to attend fall classes. When I informed my workout buddies about my newest endeavor, they were intrigued.

"You have to go see this guy, Parker," one of them said. The other guys nodded in agreement. "He has a Kenpo school just two blocks up the street from Pasadena City College."

Prologue

"You should check him out, because in Kenpo, he's the real deal."

Of course I took them up on their recommendation. I enrolled in college and once done with the enrollment process, I ventured up the street and saw Ed Parker's school in a little strip mall on Walnut Street. I walked into the studio, and the only person there was Ed Parker. I introduced myself and told him about my Hawaiian friends who I had been training with and they recommended I come to see him. He greeted me and we talked for a bit. He then insisted that I follow him onto the training floor so that he could show me some things. He did a series of movements with speed, power, and precision. The whole school shook. I had never experienced anything like that before. It was like an earthquake had shot through all of California.

As soon as he moved, I was hooked. I wanted to be able to move like him. After this brief session with Ed Parker, I told him I wanted to enroll and so I signed up right then and there. Two days later, I started taking regular classes. I drove 60 miles one way from March Air Force Base to Ed's school in Pasadena twice a week, until September. When I got out of the Air Force, I moved to Azusa CA, only 20 miles from Ed's school. That made things a little easier.

My first official lesson was with Jimmy Ibrao, one of Ed Parker's black belts. He was getting ready to teach the beginning group class that I was attending. Since I showed up early, he said, "Come out here." I entered the mats and he said, "Let me see what you got."

"What? I replied. "You mean you want me to throw some punches and kicks and stuff? You mean *at you?*"

"Yes, at me," he said.

"Like, *for real*," I asked.

"Yes, for real." He grinned.

I took a swing at him. The next thing I knew I was on the ground looking up at him. He looked down at me. "I don't want that to happen to you ever again." I eagerly agreed. Jimmy was extremely impressive, an amazingly talented martial artist.

Sometime after I started my Kenpo training, all of Ed Parker's black belts, brown belts, and a few white belts left him . . . all on the same day. They left because they were tired of doing the same material over and over again and wanted to train with the endless amount of new material offered by another Black Belt named Jimmy Woo. This was an event of truly epic proportions because it was a major catalyst that determined what came after.

After the split with Jimmy, I skipped a step ahead of the advanced class coming behind me. On Monday and Wednesdays I taught the beginning, intermediate, and advanced. Then I had a personal class from Ed Parker that fed me the material I needed to teach at the Pasadena school. Along with Chuck Sullivan and Sterling Peacock, who were covering classes on the other days and at the school, this was the way the teaching worked for some time.

The training was different back then. It was hardcore and body-breaking workouts that gave birth to the label "dungeon dojo." I have no quarrel with that description because indeed, in those days we really did train in degrees of pain. "No pain, no gain" was the prevailing methodology. Few had the fortitude to persevere in that kind of training.

In those early days there were no children and no females. Except, there was one female student I'll remember forever. Her name was Ruby, and she was just plain mean and nasty. The first time I saw her, she was sparring against one of the other male students. Suddenly, Ruby blasted this poor fool with a wicked back-knuckle strike to his eyebrow. Instant gash, instant buckets of blood, instant trip to the ER. It took six stitches to close the gash. In that one strike, Ruby managed to impress and scare the hell out of the rest of us. That girl was death on two feet.

Don't tell me females are incapable of defending themselves against a violent physical assault. I know better. Ladies, tigers don't lose sleep over the concerns of sheep. Don't be a sheep, be a Ruby.

Today, one of the self-defense workshops I teach is a little something I recall back from the 1950s. I give the students a 20-minute taste of a typical class from the early days of Kenpo. After about 20 minutes of these classes, students are starting to gasp and barf a little. Well, you get the idea. After the class, students

Prologue

came up to me and said, "I can't believe that you really used to train like this." I would reply that we actually did train like that, but did it for an-hour-and-a-half, non-stop. It was like that all the time. Then they would say things like, "God, I wish we could train like that all of the time." And I said, "No you don't. You only like it now because it's different, but if you had to do it every class, you probably would not; you probably would find some reason to drop out."

Sounds a little harsh, huh? Well maybe so, but if you're talking about being able to defend yourself in a real situation, you have to not only be as fit as you can be but also develop and maintain a level of experience and expertise with the basics. You must become an expert with the basics. If you don't do that, you won't be physically able to protect yourself or anyone else in the real world.

It is true that in the late 1950s, and up until the mid-1960s, the advanced class was not open to viewing by the general public. The door was locked!

Today, the lion's share of the knowledge contained in the American Kenpo system is digitized and can be bought by anyone. It seems strange to some that in our beginning we did not allow the public to view any of the vast material. One of the reasons we did this was because some of the beginning students who had watched the advanced class early on found the intensity troubling, and remarked, "Those guys aren't doing that to me. There's no way anyone's getting me in that class," and quit training altogether. The other reason the door was locked was back then we were hesitant about giving out material to students before their time. We wanted to make it a privilege in the sense that the student must earn the right to learn brown belt material by busting their butts through the ranks, and later, black belt material. None of the instructors wanted to make it easy. I know I didn't. I wanted my students to earn every inch of their belt, just the way I had. Anything else would rob them of the pride they deserved on the day they legitimately earned that brown or black belt.

I remember with clarity the day I made first-degree black belt. It came out of the blue, although both Ed Parker and Chuck Sullivan had been testing me for about a month prior to the actual promotion.

When Ed Parker had me kneel to receive my black belt, I didn't want to take it because it was the same color as the belt around his waist, and I didn't feel I was worthy to wear the belt the same color as Ed Parker's. What is important to note is that back then, black belts did not wear red stripes or tips on their black belts. I'll never forget Ed Parker's response to me, which was, "As your instructor, it is my place to decide when you are worthy of a black belt, not yours." I remember thinking, *now I actually have to live up to the honor and challenge of being a black belt*. My dedication was cranked up a notch or two. I was absolutely determined not to dishonor that black belt and all it stood for.

This sense of honor and commitment is to my mind an essential part of owning and operating a martial arts school. It was common back in the 1950s and 1960s that a person's word was his bond. For instance, my first Kenpo School was with Jim Thompson. We were partners on a handshake for about 10 years. I don't know that one could do that nowadays. In my travels around the Kenpo community today, I am gratified by the degree of respect and honor I saw.

I'd like to share what may well be my most special moment of my Kenpo journey. That moment occurred on the day when I realized that I had made a positive change in someone else's life.

Many years ago in the days when we were still teaching in degrees of pain it was standard operating procedure to physically crank on every student in the school. The thinking was that if you could survive the training, you'd have no problem coping with a real street situation. Good, bad, or indifferent, that's the way it was back then.

There was this one student whom I taught in those days who was the single most uncoordinated klutz that I have ever seen. He literally could not walk and chew gum at the same time. He had a problem tying his own shoelaces. For almost two years, this guy trained with me. Apparently, the only thing he could do was take a lot of punishment. Boy, did he take punishment. It seemed he was everyone's punching bag. He never missed a class. Finally, the day came when I decided to promote him to orange belt, in spite of the fact that he could barely

Prologue

get through short form one. When I promoted him to orange belt he was so shocked he couldn't speak. He left, and I didn't see him again for a few weeks.

He showed up at my office door one day to ask if he could talk to me. I said, "Sure, what's on your mind?"

"I wanted you to know that I know that you just gave me this orange belt," he replied, and then held up his hand to keep me from speaking and continued. "Dave, you know that I tried to do the best that I can. I never miss a class, and I also train and practice at home. I work hard at this, but in-spite of everything, I just can't get it. There is something about me that for some reason keeps me from being able to get it. Anyway, I wanted to tell you that I'm moving back East, and I won't be able to train here anymore. I also wanted to tell you that I will treasure this orange belt for the rest of my life. You believed in me enough to give it to me, and I have found that, for the first time in my life, I can look people in the eye."

Wow!

We said our farewells with tears in our eyes, and I never saw him again. Maybe he'll read this page and recognize this story and get in touch with me again. I sure hope so. If not, Godspeed my friend. You gave me so much more than I ever gave to you.

Looking back over the past 62 years I know that in some primal way, from the very first day Kenpo was important in my life. I knew I would be a better man if I would commit and train as hard as I could for as long as I could. As things turned out, I was right.

All-in-all, one of the best things that ever happened to me is that I gained self-confidence. I put myself on the line, and I was tested. For the most part, I received passing grades. Because I was successful at something that was pretty darn difficult to do, I ended up with a sense of realistic self-confidence. I knew I could function against heavy odds. I knew I was competent. I knew I was able to move with authority and skill. More importantly, all that training affected the rest of my life in mostly positive terms. Not long ago, an old friend observed in me what he called peacefulness. I'd like to think that what he sees is a man who today is comfortable in his own skin and doesn't have to prove anything anymore.

Chapter 1: The Beginning

The 1950s was a legendary era for music with such icons as Little Richard, Jerry Lee Lewis, Big Joe Turner, and two of my favorites—Chuck Berry and Fats Domino, whom I met up with a couple of times while working for Elvis. Although rock and roll dominated the 1950s, especially with the booming popularity of the electric guitar, I was a huge fan of jazz and swing. I remember well when Elvis came onto the scene in the mid-1950s.

There was something so different about Elvis. The religious leaders of the day thought he was the spawn of the devil. He was criticized by many due to his hip-swiveling moves when he performed. He had a sexually provocative method of entertaining that had never been seen before. Many people were disgusted by it, while others loved his rebellious behaviors.

Initially, I wasn't a fan of Elvis's music, but there was no denying that he would permanently alter the look, sound, and feel of contemporary music. His style of music was coined "rockabilly" because it was a fusion of rock and roll and country music. Other well-known icons like Jerry Lee Lewis and Buddy Holly also ventured into that realm.

Elvis continued to become more popular throughout the late 1950s. It seemed every girl was mesmerized by him and fantasized about him. They couldn't get enough of him. After a two-year stint in the military, 1958-1960, Elvis recorded some of his most popular music.

He began his movie career with *Love Me Tender* (1958). It didn't do anything for me. I thought it was okay, but nothing to get excited about. Apparently, it was well-received because after getting out of the Army in 1960, Elvis devoted most of the 1960s to acting. He took eight years off from performing live as a musician to make films.

I never got into Elvis's movies, and it had nothing to do with him. I was interested in *Frankenstein* movies and action flicks. I wasn't into the type of movies Elvis starred in. I rarely had money to spend to go see a movie at that age. When I did, I went to movies like *The Defiant Ones* (1958) and *Horror of Dracula* (1958).

In 1968, Elvis got back to performing live. He stopped making movies. He wasn't getting the roles he wanted, and he felt that the quality of his films was deteriorating. He went back to focusing on his music career. I didn't pay much attention. I was too busy with my own life, focusing on my true love, Kenpo Karate. When I was introduced to what would become my life's pride and joy, little did I know it would define my life's path and get me a job protecting Elvis.

I continued to train with Ed Parker and teach for him. In late 1962, I received my black belt. I was only the eighth person to be promoted to black belt under Ed. Aside from Rich Montgomery being the first and Jimmy Ibrao being the second, I can't remember the order of the others. The others in front of me, however, included: Joe Dimmick (who might have been Ed's third black belt), Rick Flores, Al Tracy, Jim Tracy, and Chuck Sullivan.

I knew I had to step up my game. Not that I was ever a slacker, but since I was wearing the same color around my waist as Ed Parker, I had to fit the mold. That was a huge task and a difficult one. That's exactly what I did. I continued working hard, training and teaching for Ed. I was also one of the originators of the infamous annual International Karate Championship (IKC) held in Long Beach, CA, beginning in 1964.

I was responsible for developing the set of rules for the IKCs and served as one of the Directors of the tournament in different capacities for 12 years. I was also the President of Ed Parker's International Kenpo Karate Association (IKKA) for several years. During that period I was the only other person, other than Ed Parker and his wife Leilani, to have that honor.

Ed Parker first met Elvis in late 1960 when Ed was putting on a karate demonstration for a bunch of doctors at the Beverly Wilshire Hotel in Beverly

Hills. Elvis was working on a movie and was staying in that hotel at the time. Red West, one of Elvis's bodyguards, saw an advertisement in the hotel lobby. Because of Elvis's interest and initial background in martial arts—he studied karate while he was in the Army stationed in Germany—he was intrigued and wanted to check out the demonstration.

Elvis loved the demo and introduced himself to Ed afterward, which shows how humble Elvis was. He didn't assume Ed knew who he was; who didn't know of Elvis Presley? After their brief introduction and handshake, they talked at length about martial arts. The meeting began a lifelong friendship.

Elvis constantly promoted Ed and his Kenpo studio. Elvis referred students to Ed and even introduced him to the audience during shows Ed attended. Ed eventually began protecting Elvis, but was never an employee. Ed protected him as a friend, and never wanted to be paid for it. Of course, Elvis gifted him with many expensive items over the years, including a brand new white Cadillac (on a whim), which was the norm for Elvis. Elvis loved to bless people with gifts. He did it all the time, but only when *he* felt like doing it. He had an amazing heart, but never gave when greedy people would hint about something they wanted. Elvis gave when *he* wanted to, which was often.

Chapter 2: Elvis and Martial Arts

In July 1972, one of the most special things happened to me, and I certainly did not expect it. I was sitting at my desk in my karate school in Glendora, CA, when I received a call from George Waite, one of Ed Parker's black belts, to join a group of black belt friends of mine for a workout at Ed Parker's Santa Monica Studio. I hadn't seen that group of guys in a while, so I was excited to join them for some Kenpo fun.

Shortly after my arrival, we started working out and having a lot of fun beating the crap out of one another, since Kenpo people enjoy getting slapped around. For us, if we didn't leave with a few bruises, we didn't work out. After about a half hour into our training session, there was some commotion at the door. I looked up and thought I was seeing things. Maybe I was hit a little too hard during one of the drills. To my surprise, it was real, and there *he* was. Elvis Presley, the greatest entertainer alive, with a small entourage. I don't recall who was with him. When Elvis walked into a room, he was the only person you saw. He was that powerful.

In a small state of shock, I couldn't believe I was staring at the one and only Elvis Presley. Elvis dropped by to see us. We were so excited to not only meet him but also to know that he was watching us work out. We continued our session as Elvis observed intently. After a brief time, to our surprise, Elvis stepped onto the mat to train with us. By a stroke of luck, he chose me as his training partner. Now, this was surreal. Not only was I meeting "the King" face to face, but also, I was personally training with him.

I quickly realized that Elvis was unfamiliar with the martial arts techniques we were covering. I tried to guide him through the movements without making it look obvious. I didn't want to come across as trying to tell him what to do, so I carefully worked through a strategy. Thankfully, it worked. It ended well and we all had a blast. After our training session, Elvis and I briefly talked, and he thanked me for working with him.

It's important to note that Elvis had trained in martial arts prior to this adventure, although he wasn't familiar with the Kenpo material. It would be difficult for anybody to go into a martial arts studio and pick right up on what the students were doing. It would be like me, a highly skilled 6th-degree Black Belt in Kenpo, going into a Brazilian Jiu-Jitsu school to work out with several experts, going over the rubber guard, the scissor sweep, and the baseball choke. I could probably pick-up some of that with a little help, but it would be awkward. Elvis did just fine, considering the circumstances.

Apparently, Elvis liked beating on me and appreciated my help. A few days later I received a phone call from Ed Parker. He told me Elvis really enjoyed working out with me and wanted to meet with me at his home in Beverly Hills, CA.

I said, "Are you kidding me? Certainly! Of course! When would he like to see me?" Ed arranged for him and me to visit with Elvis a few evenings later.

Ed and I drove up to Elvis's place and were welcomed in. I was more than impressed with Elvis's beautiful home. I had never seen a house as gorgeous. Of course, I grew up a poor kid in a tenement with no phone, no TV, no car, no hot water, and only one bathroom to accommodate my mom, dad, and four brothers.

Once Ed and I were in Elvis's home hanging out, he came down to meet us. We spent some time getting to know one another, talking about everything under the sun and laughing a lot. After an hour or so, Elvis excused himself. He and the guys had to take care of something outside. Elvis, Ed Parker, and the rest of the guys left me sitting there looking around and wondering what was happening. Shortly after, I heard Elvis call for me from outside, asking me to come out and join them. I thought maybe there was some trouble.

I quickly went outside. Everyone was standing around this beautiful little dark blue 1971 Mercedes Benz 280 SL parked in the driveway. Elvis then said, "Dave, I got this little problem I'd like you to help me with."

"Sure Elvis. What can I do?"

"It's this car," he said. "It's cluttering up my driveway. I want you to drive it away."

"Sure Elvis. Where do you want me to drive it?"

"Anywhere you want. The car is yours." He then handed me some papers and the keys.

I was stunned. I didn't know what to say. As you might imagine I struggled to understand that Elvis had just given me a car. I choked up and said some words of gratitude to which Elvis just laughed. "Enjoy the car, Dave." He said goodnight, and he and the other guys went inside, leaving Ed Parker and me to drive our respective cars home.

I proudly drove that beautiful car home. The next day I went to the DMV to register it. They asked me what I paid for it, I presume so that they could charge me more. When I told them that I paid nothing for it, it was a gift from Elvis Presley, they didn't quite know what to do. The clerk was just thrilled that I knew Elvis and started telling the other clerks, who were equally impressed. I was officially the proud owner of a new gorgeous Mercedes Benz.

A few years later, it got vandalized. Some punks came in, scratched it all up, broke into the trunk, and stole my golf clubs and a toolbox that contained several tools. After it was vandalized, I had it repainted silver. It was the metal flake kind of paint, so it glistened. It was a $2,000 paint job, plus having to replace my golf clubs and my toolbox. Luckily, my insurance paid for it all.

After Elvis gave me that car and I drove it home, he and I had several conversations over the phone and met up in person a few times within the next six months. Then one day he took the time to drive out to my studio in Glendora and presented me with one of his personal gold *TCB* necklaces. TCB stood for "taking care of business," which was Elvis's motto.

Elvis presented the TCB necklaces to only his closest companions. I was beyond flattered. Now I was a part of his inner circle. It was such an amazing feeling that Elvis Presley, *the* Elvis Presley, thought so highly of me after our initial training session and our meetings. He took the time to come out and present me with such an amazing gift. I loved the necklace, but more importantly, I loved the close friendship I had with such a caring man.

That wasn't even the best part of the day for me. After talking with Elvis briefly, as I held my TCB necklace, he asked me to become one of his bodyguards. I couldn't believe it. If I accepted, I would be employed by the biggest musical icon ever. Not that I had to think about it, or anything. I would've been a complete fool to turn him down. Not to mention, I had just gotten divorced, and it would be a wonderful way to meet women.

Now that I was a part of the "Memphis Mafia" as we were called, I began teaching Kenpo to Elvis and his other bodyguards. They had trained with Ed Parker sporadically, but once I was hired I began teaching them on a regular basis. Elvis had many lessons from me throughout the four years I protected him. He was mostly interested in working individual basic moves. I showed him many techniques, each of which had several moves. He would mimic me in the air and then do them on a partner. He was more interested in single basic moves than the full techniques.

Elvis took lessons with me until he got tired, then sat down to observe the rest of the lesson. Many times I'd be teaching Red and Sonny West, and Elvis would sit in. It was never anything formal. We didn't have specific days or times when we trained. It happened in various places and times under different circumstances.

We'd be on tour, and I'd give Elvis a lesson in the hotel room. The lessons were never long. Elvis didn't have the stamina to work out for an extended period. His life was difficult with all the concerts, his odd sleep schedule, and with the pills he was taking. I never promoted Elvis in Kenpo. All of Elvis's promotions were directly under Ed Parker, though I signed the certificates.

Ed Parker promoted Elvis to 8th-degree black belt on September 5, 1974. That same day, at the same time, I was promoted to 7th-degree black belt. Many people have wondered how a student could have a higher rank than his instructor, but he was one degree higher than I in rank on that day. It didn't bother me. I taught Elvis because he wanted me to teach him. His rank was between him and Ed Parker. I had nothing to do with that.

Ed Parker came up to me a few days later and said, "You know if you want, I'll make you an 8th." I told him that there was no way I would accept it. Apparently, he felt I was upset that my student was ranked higher than I was in the system that I knew a thousand times better than he. I understood the circumstances, and I didn't want to get a rank under those conditions. Besides, he just promoted me to 7th three days prior. That wouldn't look good at all.

If that wasn't interesting enough, one year later, Ed Parker promoted Elvis to a 9th-degree black belt without me knowing about it. Ed had my signature on a rubber stamp. He could just stamp my signature on the certificates. With that said, it happened unbeknownst to me.

The reason I know Elvis was promoted to 9th-degree black belt under Ed Parker was that, years after Elvis died, I was contacted by a girl Elvis was dating at the time of his passing. She had a copy of the certificate and wanted to sell it. She sent me a picture of it; I looked at it, stunned. I had no clue Ed had promoted Elvis to 9th. Most people in Kenpo thought Ed Parker promoted only up to 7th-degree black belt.

The truth is Ed promoted Elvis to 8th and 9th black for his own reasons. The word "honorary" was not on any of those certificates; neither was an expiration date. Those are the cold, hard facts.

Over the years, there have been numerous articles about Elvis and his involvement in the martial arts. Many have chosen to portray Elvis as an extraordinarily dynamic and talented martial artist with world-class abilities. Although I have no quarrel with those writers, I was Elvis's personal bodyguard and Kenpo instructor for four years. I knew Elvis well, and I know Kenpo even better.

Frankly, I am uniquely qualified to comment on the fact of the matter with respect to Elvis and his martial arts skills.

Several people have asked me about my own background in the martial arts world, and what gives me the authority to render an opinion on anybody's martial arts skills? Martial Arts are my primary profession and have been for over 60 years. I have been a martial artist and self-defense instructor since 1958. Sometimes it was full-time and sometimes it was part-time, but I've been doing it a long time.

In the martial arts world, I am an American Kenpo karate stylist. There are many styles of martial arts, even different styles within styles. For instance, when you say 'karate' it's like saying car or automobile. What kind of car? A Ford Mustang? A Chevy Corvette? A Dodge Viper? Or did you mean truck? What kind of truck? A Ford Ranger? A Chevy Silverado? A Dodge Ram? I'm sure you get the point. There are all kinds of vehicles. Likewise, there are all kinds of karate.

As I mentioned, my style of karate is American Kenpo and I have my own organization called Dave Hebler's Kenpo Karate Association (DHKKA). Under the auspices of my organization, I am a 10th-degree Black Belt, the highest belt in any martial art. In the American Kenpo world, I am the second-most senior black belt in the world. I'm extremely proud of that.

You may find it interesting that in the early 1960s, Bruce Lee used to come around and work out with us at Ed Parker's studio in Pasadena. I had the opportunity to spar with Bruce on a few occasions, and that was an interesting experience. He clocked me a few times. I hit him a few times. Our sparring matches were even. Neither of us dominated.

When I sparred with Bruce Lee, not many people knew him yet. Nobody knew what a phenomenon he would become. The martial arts world owes Bruce Lee a great deal of appreciation for what he did for it. He is probably the most iconic martial artist who ever lived. Elvis Presley also did so much for the martial arts, especially Ed Parker's American Kenpo.

Bruce Lee was not a big influence on my own martial arts journey. He pointed out certain aspects of the material (technique, mostly) that he thought could be improved, and he took the time to explain his reasoning to me, which I appreciated. Working techniques and sparring with him was a fun time for both of us.

It's important that people understand that almost always when we were working out together in the *dojo;* it was not a blood sport. It was training and learning experience for both me and Bruce Lee. We'd beat each other up on the mats and then go have a beer.

Elvis played his guitar on stage with a sticker of the IKKA crest on it. People could stare at the patch of Ed Parker's organization while Elvis sang some of his hits. The funny thing was that Elvis' guitar was mostly a prop. He randomly strummed some chords, but most of the time, he just had the guitar on him. He really wasn't a good guitar player. He was decent on the piano, but just basic on the guitar.

Aside from having that sticker on his guitar, Elvis would do martial arts moves on the stage during his performances. He also went to some tournaments, even though pandemonium ensued whenever he showed up.

Elvis couldn't walk into a donut shop without people going berserk, because nobody ever looked at Elvis and said, "You look kind of familiar." No, they instantly recognized him and went insane. It is difficult for me to put into words what that was really like. Unless you were there, you just don't have an experience quite like that. He was such a phenomenon. He was the single most popular human being on the face of the planet at one time. I feel he is the most popular human being ever, but that's subjective.

Elvis's approval of anything was an endorsement beyond belief. Even the fans of today know Elvis had affection for martial arts. If somebody today knows that Elvis was involved with the martial arts that should answer any question you have about how he affected the martial arts world.

I don't believe anybody would argue that Elvis Presley was the greatest entertainer of all time. Nobody rated with him in that department. He brought joy and happiness to millions of people. Elvis, the person, was one of the warmest and most generous people in the world in many ways. He was gregarious and funny, often hilariously so. He was the most down-to-earth person I have ever known. He was so fun to be around that he just lit up the room every time he was present. He was deeply caring and genuinely loved his family, friends, and fans.

Elvis truly loved his fans. He always wanted to put on the best show for them. He appreciated them and their support. During his concerts, he would often show off both of his hands full of rings—like a quarter of a million dollars' worth—and he'd say to the audience, "I want to thank you very much. You made it possible for me to have all these jewels." He really meant it. He had all the patience in the world with his fans. He never said, "Leave me alone." He would listen intently to them, reply to them, and talk with them.

Although Elvis was the greatest entertainer ever, he wasn't the greatest martial artist ever. To my knowledge, he never trained on a regular basis in any style, or with a single instructor, in his entire adult life. He did have sporadic lessons and even some semi-regular lessons with different instructors over the years, but nothing on a long-term basis. Not because he didn't want to, but because he couldn't. His fame got in the way. Everybody knew who Elvis was. When people saw him they just screamed as tears of joy ran down their faces.

You can understand why Elvis couldn't attend regular classes at a local martial arts school; not without a riot breaking out, that is. There were some great martial arts instructors, however, who thought Elvis was good enough to be awarded a black belt. Who am I to argue with their decisions?

Both Ed Parker and I agreed that Elvis had the potential to be a great martial artist. He had a good physique for most of his life. With proper dieting and training, he could've had a great physique. He had access to the finest trainers and instructors in the world and could've trained on a private basis with them as he did with Ed Parker and me. Training on a private basis is only part of the equation, however.

For a student to really excel he must train with other students and compete in adversarial situations with a variety of trained individuals. That option was not available to Elvis as a practical matter because he couldn't risk getting injured. Besides, who cares about whether Elvis was the greatest martial artist who ever lived? I certainly don't, and neither should anyone else.

There is no question that Elvis loved martial arts and was a dedicated supporter his entire adult life. In fact, he was so enthusiastic about martial arts in general, and particularly Kenpo, that he started his own martial arts organization with me as one of the directors. Unfortunately, he never lived to see his martial arts dreams become a reality. The organization never panned out. He never even named it. The genesis of that organization is found within Elvis's funding of the "Gladiators" project, which ended up being two separate entities: one was the "Gladiators;" the other was the "New Gladiators," which came out first.

George Waite originated the idea for the project. Through Ed Parker, George brought the idea to Elvis, who gave George a lot of money to start it. George began filming footage at tournaments. The original film footage is still out there. It's owned by Rich Hale. I'm in some of the footage, mostly as a referee, as are several of my students.

Ed Parker took a team of fighters over to Europe to fight some of the European martial artists. The members of the U.S. team included Tom Kelly, Benny Urquidez, Ron Marchini, Darnell Garcia, John Natividad, and Roy Kurban. They had special uniforms made that mimicked Elvis's flare-type pants that he wore on stage. All of that was also a part of the "New Gladiators," which Elvis planned on turning into a feature film and would pay me and everybody else $50,000. Unfortunately, it didn't happen.

That footage bounced around for years and nobody did anything with it until Rising Sun Productions came out with the "New Gladiators" DVD, which shows some great history of some of the best karate fighters of all time. The

DVD focuses on Team USA fighting at Wembley Stadium in London, England, and then the next day, fighting in Brussels against its best fighters.

Aside from Elvis displaying his skills, I displayed mine quite a bit as well. Both of us demonstrated on Red West. Elvis also demonstrated on David Stanley, his stepbrother. Elvis was attempting to show how you can hit with multiple strikes and showing different lethal assaults to targets. He also showed how to defend against a weapon, primarily a revolver. Then he demonstrated his *Chi*. Red put his fist right on Elvis's throat and Elvis pressed forward, knocking Red all the way across the room. Elvis then had Red punch him as hard as he could in the ribs, three times in a row. Elvis didn't even wince.

At one point during that demo, Elvis promoted Bill Wallace and gave him a trophy. In Kenpo, when you get promoted, you get kicked in the stomach by the person who promoted you. Elvis kicked a little low and accidentally hit Bill in the balls. Bill took it well. I had to kick Bill next, so I made sure to hit directly in his stomach and didn't hit him hard. I was embarrassed that Elvis did that. It was mortifying. I gritted my teeth and smiled. Bill is a tough dude. He sucked it up, but that shouldn't have happened. None of that footage was in "New Gladiators." It was put into a separate DVD "Gladiators," which can be found on Amazon for over $100. There is a lot of footage of me, Red West, Bill Wallace, and Elvis in "Gladiators."

Ed Parker wasn't present during the demo. He was almost never around during the four years I protected Elvis. Ed called me every day, however, to check up on things. It was the perfect solution for Ed to have me, his right-hand man, taking care of the situation. He had a lot on his plate.

The demo I put on at Kang Rhee's school never got filmed. It was in front of 150-200 people who had never seen Kenpo before. I put on one hell of a demo and slapped the shit out of Red West. He was a tough guy so he took it well. You could hear people in the audience go *Ouch* as they winced in agony. They couldn't believe what they were seeing. If I had started my own studio the next day, I would have had 150-200 students immediately.

In the late 1960s and into the late 1970s, whenever a Kenpo student at an IKKA member school made rank in a black belt category, the student was awarded a gold-plated ID card sized to fit into a wallet. Elvis loved them. He carried one of those gold ID cards in his wallet every time he was awarded a new black belt ranking by the chairman of the board, Ed Parker.

Elvis was so proud of his card that he would show it to anyone, anywhere, anytime. At his request, I created 100 copies of his 8th-degree black belt card so he could hand them out to select family and friends. He did indeed pass out a few; the remainder stayed in my possession. Over the years I sold a few and gave away a few others. Several years ago, I had 200 more copies made. I still have them.

Elvis loved those cards so much that one day he asked me to make up another gold ID card, which would be for the Elvis Presley Show. He planned to pass them out to everyone in the show and those in his personal entourage to keep as a memento. I told him that I would, of course. I asked him to write his signature on a piece of paper, and I would design one for him. He gave me his signature, I designed the card, he approved it, and I had 100 copies made. Just like with the IKKA gold ID card, Elvis gave away only a few of the Elvis Presley Show gold ID cards and I retained the rest. I still have many of them as well.

As for the TCB necklace Elvis presented me the day he asked me to be his bodyguard, years later, long after Elvis's death, I ended up selling it to a guy who was looking for Elvis memorabilia. I sold it to him for $3,000. A week later I got an offer from a collector in Europe for $25,000 for the necklace. I went back to the guy I sold it to. "Listen, you want to sell that necklace, because I got a person who will buy it for 25 grand." It came as no surprise that he wasn't interested.

Part of Elvis's overall mission with the martial arts organization he was forming, that I was to be a part of, was a self-defense program for women. He and I discussed what kind of material we would put into the curriculum. Elvis knew how important a self-defense program for women was to me. I wanted to get more training specifically for women. Back in those days, women in the martial arts were rare. There weren't many, and the material didn't suit them well. The existing material didn't relate to women because they have unique self-defense needs. I wanted to emphasize training specifically for women that would uniquely address their needs.

Chapter 3: My First Assignment – Lake Tahoe

The first time I ever saw Elvis perform live was during my initial stint as his bodyguard. I was backstage at Sahara Tahoe in Lake Tahoe in 1972. Lake Tahoe is one of the most beautiful places on earth. It's a large freshwater lake right on the state line between California and Nevada, and is a major tourist attraction. The shoreline contains several parks, beaches, swimming areas, and other attractions. It's a three-hour drive around the 72-mile lake, if all you do is drive.

I was talking with the other guys backstage while Elvis did his infamous intro. Then he went out to begin the show. I was stunned, like I got hit by a hammer. I could not believe how good he really was. It was the first time I had witnessed his dancing and strutting around on stage. It was like he was in a trance, and nothing could get him out of it.

The way Elvis mesmerized the crowd was unbelievable. It was like I was dreaming as I gazed at the thousands of roaring fans, many of them crying, as they got a glimpse of their hero. The way Elvis moved, his amazing voice, his gleaming charisma, and his sense of humor were infectious. I became an instant fan right then and there. He was astounding.

Thousands of flashbulbs blinked on and off above the 22,000 screaming fans in the sold-out arena. It was absolute mayhem with the energy escalating with every passing second. At first, hundreds of young women rushed the stage; seconds later, hundreds of older women rushed the stage. The glow radiating off Elvis made it seem like a spiritual experience. That wasn't the Elvis I knew; this Elvis was an icon—a god. The hair on the back of my neck stood up as Elvis's unmatchable charisma shot through the crowd's insanity. I was overwhelmed. I knew I would never look at Elvis the same way again.

I was so captivated by the experience that I asked Colonel Parker, his manager, backstage if Elvis's concerts were always like that.

"Dave, you've got to understand something," the Colonel responded. "This is not a concert. Anytime the King of Rock 'n Roll gets on stage, it's not really a concert. It's a historical event." I thought about that for a second and realized my future would include many more historical events.

The next morning, I got cleaned up and headed down to the restaurant to meet up with some of the guys for breakfast. It was 9:00 a.m. and, as the elevator door opened, a line of people, four abreast, stretched as far as the eye could see, all the way onto the casino floor, all around the outside of the casino, back across the middle of the casino, and up to the showroom floor. I couldn't believe my eyes. Six good-looking cocktail waitresses served the entire line.

Holy crap! What the hell is this? I thought. You could hardly get through the place. As I was wondering why there were so many people standing in a line at least a mile long, I heard someone shout my name. I turned around and noticed a friend standing in the line. "What are you doing?" I asked.

"We're in line for the show," he replied.

"Is there a matinee?" I thought maybe there was a noon show.

"No tonight's show. At eight o'clock."

I couldn't believe that the line for the 8:00 p.m. show was as long as it was, and it was only 9:00 a.m. I had never seen anything like it.

"Listen, could you help us out?" my friend asked.

"What do you mean?" I asked.

"You know, can you get us to the front of the line?"

"I don't think I can, frankly." This was my second day on the job, and I didn't know what I could or couldn't do. My main concern was protecting Elvis. I didn't know what kind of perks I could provide as part of Elvis's entourage.

My friend held up some rolled-up bills in his hand. "Here, let me help you with your decision."

"No, I'll help you, regardless," I replied, glancing at that wad of cash. "If I can help you, I will."

"There's $300 there," he said.

"I realize that, but I don't think I can help you. Let me find out if I can do something." In the restaurant, I went over to some of the guys in our group. I explained the situation. One of them told me to bring my friend and his guest to the front of the line and introduce them to the maître d'.

I went back and told my friend, "I'll take you and your guest to the front of the line. You need to hand the maître d' that $300 and the maître d will take care of you." I quickly realized that they take care of people who slip them cash. Apparently, it happened quite often.

Not only were those shows all sold out, but they sold tickets for people to sit on the floor and on the stairs. They packed them in there like sardines. I later found out that the maître d' at the Hilton in Vegas had bought his job for $500,000. That's how much money they made. The new maître d' paid the old maître d' that kind of money to take over the job. The head parking attendant at the Hilton in Vegas made $75,000 a year. We are talking in the early 1970s.

That began my adventure as one of Elvis's bodyguards. It was surreal, and many more interesting situations were to come. Suddenly, everybody knew everything about me. Fans knew I had children, my date of birth, and the wine I preferred, and even my favorite color. It was truly mind-boggling.

I really hit it off with the other members of Elvis's entourage. I didn't know any of them until I started working for him. My relationship with them was good at first, but got even better each year. We worked well together. We all shared a common goal, to protect Elvis. I especially got along well with Red West. He and I had some great conversations and some amazing times. He was a wonderful man.

Initially, I worked part-time for Elvis. After that first concert, I traveled with him, on and off for a couple years before going full-time. Between tours, I would either stay with Elvis at Graceland or go to California to be with my family. Each situation was different. The four bodyguards—Red, Sonny, Dick Grob, a former police officer, and I—would often work two on, two off, when not on tour, so we could get some quality time with our families. When we were on tour, all four of us worked 24/7.

Interestingly, years later, I lived at Lake Tahoe for a few years working as a pit boss/assistant day shift manager at the Tahoe Biltmore Hotel and Casino. Although I had been there several times with Elvis, I learned a lot more about Lake Tahoe once I lived there. For instance, it is the second-most pristine large body of freshwater in the world. With respect to its pristine condition, it's largely due to a joint California/Nevada environmental group called the TRPA (Tahoe Regional Planning Agency), which is charged with ensuring that the original nature of the lake stays that way.

The TRPA has enormous power and is as serious as a heart attack. As an example, I applied to remove a couple of dead trees from my property and was flat-out turned down. TRPA warned me, "Don't do it on the sly, because the fine will go a long way toward putting you into bankruptcy." The lesson learned was, you'd best not contribute any kind of pollution to the lake or you will be one sorry individual.

There is enough water in the lake to cover the entire state of California 14 and 1/2 inches deep, and to cover the entire state of Texas nine inches deep. Although the air temperature in the winter goes as low as 25° below zero, the lake has never been known to freeze over. It has its own species of fish, and they spawn. There's a viewing area on the west shore where you can see them swimming upstream. It's a beautiful sight.

Just a foot or so below the surface, the temperature of the water is just a little above freezing, and remains that way clear to the bottom (close to 2000 feet). Gardnerville, NV, where I reside, is at 4750 feet elevation. The lake's surface is at 6000 feet, and the bottom of the lake is some 900 feet below me. Lake Tahoe has the reputation of 'never giving up its dead'. Apparently, a body in the lake never develops any gases because of the cold, and therefore, never rises to the surface.

You could bump someone off, dump the body in the lake, and it's gone forever. Quite handy for a hitman, isn't it?

The lake was not caused by volcanic action. It was mostly created by earthquakes; the water came from snow and rain. The Lake Tahoe area is also a large ski attraction. At one point, it was one of the largest ski areas in the world.

Then you have the infamous Donner Party, which you can look up if you aren't familiar with it. Living in the area for a few years, I always thought that those who died did so at the Donner Pass summit (8000+ feet), but they didn't. They died on the shores of Donner Lake, the elevation of which is a mere 4500 feet. Some of those who died were famously eaten by the survivors. Right next to Donner Lake is the small town of Truckee and the gateway to Lake Tahoe via Broadway Road.

There are two exits to Truckee from the freeway which ends up in Reno, NV. Coming back from a jaunt to Grass Valley, CA, I took the first off ramp into Truckee instead of my usual route. I wanted to buy something in the town of Truckee. As I made the turnoff, I noticed a sign indicating the Donner Party Memorial off to the right, close to the shores of Donner Lake. Intrigued, I checked it out.

The memorial was quite interesting and informative, but what jumped out at me the most was the obelisk that was part of the exhibit. This structure is 47 feet tall, the depth of the snow that trapped the Donner Party. Can you imagine traveling by covered-wagon and having to deal with snow 47 feet deep? With snow that deep, no edible creatures were out and about. There was no food, and no way to get any. The only available edibles were the flesh of those who died.

Lake Tahoe is one of my favorite places on the planet. I spent many weekends there protecting Elvis, which led to me moving there years later. My first venture there was just as mesmerizing as my first time watching Elvis perform, and both happened in the same weekend.

Chapter 4: Fun with Elvis

I had many delightful times with Elvis. He was such a great guy with a wonderful personality, and he truly loved the people in his circle. We had a lot of fun. Sometimes it didn't start out to be an exciting time, but it ended up being a blast. This chapter will cover some personal stories with Elvis that exemplify the term fun, in one way or another.

THE BIG DRUG BUST: I was sitting downstairs in Graceland one day when I heard Elvis on the intercom saying "Hey, Dave."

"What?"

"Come up here."

"Okay." I went up the stairs and walked into Elvis's room. A man I'd never seen before stood there. I was ready to take the guy out, but I wasn't sure why Elvis had called me to come up. I had to think quickly. I read Elvis's body language; he seemed relaxed. Things might be fine.

Elvis introduced me to the guy. It turned out he was a narcotics officer.

Elvis was fascinated with police officers in general, narcotics officers in particular (which is ironic because of Elvis's problem with prescription drugs). Elvis pulled me aside and said, "We're going on a drug bust."

I thought he was joking. I said in a sarcastic tone, "We're going on a drug bust, huh?"

"Yeah, for real," Elvis responded. "We're going to kill some bad guys."

"Yeah, okay. You mean I'm going to kill the bad guys and you're gonna watch, right?" I still thought he was joking. It seriously had to have been a colossal joke they were playing on me. The biggest reason was twofold: 1) Elvis was always playing jokes on us; and 2) We were in Memphis, Tennessee, and Elvis was wearing a snowmobile outfit, complete with a hood with two holes for the eyes and one for the mouth. He looked like a thug, completely covered up, with a cigar sticking out of his mouth. He was quite the sight.

"Why are you dressed like that?" I asked, trying not to laugh.

"I don't want anyone to recognize me."

"Elvis, it's the middle of summer in Memphis. It's hot and humid, and you're going out in public wearing a snowmobile outfit! You don't think anybody will notice?"

"Dave, they won't know it's me."

"The dog knows it's you. Everybody is going to know it's you." He looked totally ridiculous.

Nevertheless, off we went in an unmarked police car. At that point, I was still thinking it was a massive joke he was playing on me. We were always messing around with the police, and they were always fooling around with us. We ended up at the police station, where Elvis went off, looking hard at a few prisoners. I finally realized this was serious. They weren't joking. Elvis was strutting around like he was an officer mean-mugging the hooligans in the joint.

I pulled the narcotics officer aside and said, "Are you out of your mind?"

"Excuse me!" he replied.

"You are going to take Elvis and me on a real drug bust?"

"Yeah."

"What do you think is going to happen to you and your career if Elvis gets hurt?" He looked stunned. I continued, "I'm Elvis's bodyguard. It's my job to keep him safe and see that he doesn't get hurt. You better figure out how to cancel this thing and you better do it fast, because I'm telling you that this is going to be bad. Nothing good can come from this."

"Yeah, I guess you're right," he said. "I'll take care of it."

When Elvis came back in, the officer said, "I'm sorry Elvis, but the drug bust is off. It's not coming down, so we can't do it."

Elvis was totally disappointed, and I was completely elated. Elvis was obsessed with going on that drug bust. He didn't think about any possible repercussions, but I did. It was my job to think ten steps ahead of the game.

Elvis's safety was my primary priority, and nothing was going to come in the way of that, even if Elvis would be upset. We went back to Graceland and that was the end of that. Thankfully, I was never put in that position again. I was, however, put in many other situations with Elvis where I had to think fast to save the day. I guess that's why I was getting paid the big bucks.

THE SAN DIEGO CHICKEN: San Diego, CA has a professional baseball team called the Padres; as with every professional sports team in the world, it has a team mascot. The Padres' mascot is a chicken. Well, a guy dressed as one, anyway. There's nothing like wearing a giant chicken outfit on a hot Southern California day in July. I don't know why the Padres chose a chicken as their mascot, but, improbable as it may seem, it was genius.

During Padres baseball games, the San Diego Chicken made everybody laugh with its outrageous actions. It was known for hilarious physical comedy. For instance, one time, between innings, it went out to the second base umpire, got on one knee holding a towel, and motioned for the umpire to put one foot up on its knee for a shoeshine. The umpire did so and the San Diego Chicken went to town shoe-shining. Then it motioned for the other shoe, and it cleaned that one. After cleaning the shoes, the San Diego Chicken gestured that it wanted to be paid. The umpire didn't comply, so the chicken threw a fit. It started with an oversized foot scraping dirt onto the shoes it had just shined.

When the umpire gave the chicken the high sign to get out of the game, it got down on both knees and put its hands together, begging to be allowed to stay. The chicken repeatedly kissed the umpire's shoes and then his ass. The umpire shook his head a couple times, so the chicken came to his feet and "argued" with the umpire. The umpire picked the chicken up over his shoulder and carried him toward the dugout, where he dropped him in the grass. The chicken got up and stomped off the field, disgusted. That's one example of how funny the San Diego Chicken was doing its shtick.

You really had to be there to appreciate this story as much as I do but, to preface this, just picture a giant three-colored chicken. That should be funny enough.

Elvis was in the middle of a performance. He was rocking out with one of his upbeat songs, while the band was tearing it up, and the fans were going wild. It was your normal over-the-top Elvis concert: Elvis, swiveling his hips, lifting his upper lip, throwing a few martial arts moves in. Suddenly, he stopped dead in his tracks. He stopped moving, stopped singing, and just stared out into the audience.

The San Diego Chicken was dancing in the aisle. Elvis spotted the chicken and was dumbfounded. Without thinking, Elvis said into the microphone, "It's a chicken. It's a fucking chicken." The entire audience and everyone on stage began cracking up. Not just because of how funny the chicken was, but also because of Elvis's reaction.

The audience all laughed hysterically as the San Diego Chicken mimicked Elvis's dance moves. It was a riot. The chicken swiveled its hips, slapped its tail feathers, and moved its arms like Elvis. It even attempted some karate kicks, which was one of the funniest things you could ever imagine. The fans loved every second of it. Several fans gave it high fives as Elvis went back to his performance.

As if that wasn't funny enough, once the show was over, we were all laughing about the chicken and talking about what a riot it was. Elvis began imitating the chicken dancing. It was one of the funniest things I ever saw Elvis do. He seriously looked exactly like the chicken, the way he was moving his body. That was a moment I will never forget.

CHAMPAGNE, CHAMPAGNE, AND MORE CHAMPAGNE: One of greatest people I knew, who were part of Elvis's entourage for years, was Lamar Fike. I loved that guy and miss him dearly. Lamar was a big man. At one point, he weighed 400 pounds. We had so many adventures hanging out together. Here is one of the most memorable ones.

Tom Jones, the great Welsh singer and entertainer, was close friends with Elvis, and became friends with all of us. Tom was well known, not only for his talent as a performer, but also for his ability to drink champagne like it was water. It was a yearly tradition: Tom and Lamar would get together for a champagne drinking contest. It was the super-bowl of champagne guzzling.

One year in Las Vegas, I happened to have front row seats for this epic battle between two world-class champagne drinkers, and what a battle it was. With the fans cheering their chosen hero on, the contestants bellied up to the bar at the Las Vegas Hilton, and the classic encounter began. I kid you not, after a two-hour binge; each of them had consumed 17 bottles of champagne. The conversations between the two were as intense as the competition itself. It was like two professional fighters during pre-fight interviews, trashing each other profusely. Let's just say the alcohol was talking. It was hilarious. Elvis would stop and watch for a few moments, shake his head, then laugh his way back to his suite.

The big question: who won? When it was all said and done, Lamar stepped down from the barstool and promptly passed out. If you've never seen a 400-pound man pass out, I can assure you, it's a sight to behold. He dropped like a bear that just got tranquilized. He seemed to fall in slow motion. It's hard to believe that a man that big could fall so gracefully.

As soon as Lamar went down, I knew it would take an army to be able to get him back to his room. We called for a stretcher. As I suspected, it took six of us to pick him up and put him on the stretcher. After mustering Lamar back to his room, I went back to the bar to check on Tom Jones. He simply stepped down from his barstool, slightly adjusted his belt, let out a little burp, and walked away grinning. "Thank you very much," he said.

THE LADY NINJA: We were back in San Diego. There must be something in the water because we had some interesting times in San Diego. When we were on tour, we always hired local police officers to assist us with security while traveling throughout the city and at the actual venue. It was vital that local law enforcement come on board because they knew their town. They knew the ins and outs and the best way to get around the city.

We always had a great relationship with police officers. Back in those days, the police in San Diego were not allowed to moonlight, or work a second job. We hired private security to be up close and personal with us. Our instructions to them were simple: their job was to be in the front and sides of the stage, and without hurting anyone, keep fans from jumping on the stage. We strongly emphasized "without hurting anyone." We told them that if any fan gets past them, just let the fan go. Red, Sonny, Dick, and I would take care of him or her.

Normally, our plan worked well. However, this was San Diego, and things didn't go exactly as planned. The concert was in full swing and lights were strobing; fans were screaming, Elvis was performing, great as ever. Suddenly, a girl jumped up and ran toward the stage. I could tell she was serious; she looked like she was running to collect back alimony from her deadbeat ex-husband.

As the woman rushed the stage, one of the private security officers jumped out in front of her, spreading his arms and legs like he was making a snow angel in the air. The girl halted for a split-second and without hesitation blasted the officer with a swift kick to the nuts. He fell to the ground clutching his groin and rolled up into a little ball. I was astounded, but I must be honest, I think I fell in love. That's my kind of girl. In fact, I laughed my ass off as I watched that girl kick that guy's bean bag like a soccer ball.

The girl seemed shocked at what she had just accomplished. She hesitated; taking in her victory, then came back to reality. She saw me standing on the stage and didn't know what to do. She hesitated. No matter how I felt, Elvis was my main priority. She was only a few feet away from me and the stage. I gave her a nod and helped her up on the stage, so she could get a scarf from Elvis.

What can I say? I was amazed how beautiful that kick was. I admired her instinctual expertise. One of the other guys grabbed her and hustled her off the stage opposite me.

I often wonder what happened to her. We would've been a great team.

THE GAUDY BAUBLE: Elvis had an enormous number of spectacular pieces of jewelry. One of those amazing pieces was a 40-carat natural star ruby surrounded by 14 beautiful diamonds set in 18-carat gold. The thing was huge. If I remember correctly, it weighed 4.5 ounces. I called it the "gaudy bauble."

One-day, Elvis, Linda Thompson, his new girlfriend, Marty Lacker, a key member of the entourage, and I got on a plane to fly to Memphis to see how the work on the *Lisa Marie* airplane was coming along. We were enjoying our flight, chatting with one another, as always. I couldn't stop staring at the gigantic ring on Elvis's finger. I had to say something. "Elvis that is the gaudiest ring I have ever seen in my life. That thing is huge."

"You think so?" he asked.

"Yeah, can I see it?" I asked.

"Sure," he said.

He took it off and handed it to me. I put it on and said, "Wow, if you hit somebody with this, it would really leave a mark." When I said that, I was thinking about the old comic book character "The Phantom." For those who aren't familiar, "The Phantom" wore a skull and crossbones ring. When he punched somebody in the forehead with it, it would leave an indelible mark of the skull and crossbones. That's just what popped into my head as I was throwing punches in the air with the ring on like I was getting ready for a championship bare-knuckle boxing match.

Elvis started laughing. "Look at this fool. He's wearing a $50,000 ring, and he wants to hit somebody with it."

"Oh my god," I said as I came to my senses, realizing the ring I was wearing cost more than most houses. "Here," I said, removing the ring from my finger to hand back to Elvis. As I was handing the top-heavy ring back to him, I dropped it. *Good Lord, what a klutz!* I thought.

Elvis laughed even harder. "And then the fool throws it on the ground. Just keep it, Dave."

"What?" I asked, thinking I didn't hear him right.

«Keep it, Dave. It›s yours.»

"Oh, Elvis, you don't have to do that."

"I know," he replied, "But I want you to have it under one condition: you can sell that ring if you want, but as long as you own it, you can't let anyone else wear it."

"Okay," I said.

Years later, I was a dealer and pit boss at a casino. I worked at several casinos in Nevada over a 15-year span. I worked in Sparks, Lake Tahoe, Laughlin, Las Vegas, and Minden throughout my time as a dealer. I wore that ring the entire time. It was the best conversation piece I ever had; it always started a dialog between me and the customers, which led to more tokes, more commonly known as tips. I told everybody the story about Elvis and how he gifted me the ring. The story always intrigued people and made my wallet a little heavier.

I ended up selling the ring to the owner of the Elvis-A-Rama Museum in Las Vegas, where it was put on display. I sold it for $32,000, along with some other stuff. One night there was a robbery. The thief stole 10-12 pieces of jewelry, including the "gaudy bauble." The robber was caught a year later and all the jewelry was recovered. The thief had tried to sell the jewelry to an Elvis Tribute Artist, who turned him into the cops. The insurance company had already paid (much less than what the jewelry was worth), so they now owned the items. The company may still have them because I have never seen any of them in anyone's collection.

THE GUNSLINGER: The stories I am about to tell are on one hand serious, but also funny as hell. For some reason, Elvis was infatuated with guns. I quickly learned that he would randomly shoot them at anything that caught his fancy. He loved all kinds of guns, especially handguns—pistols and revolvers.

The first time I saw Elvis fire at a random target was at the Las Vegas Hilton one early afternoon. We were in the penthouse where Elvis was on the couch watching TV while having breakfast. I was sitting on the arm of the couch right next to him, just chatting away with him while he was eating. We were laughing and having an enjoyable conversation, when Robert Goulet, a singer Elvis didn't care for, came on the screen. Elvis glared at the television.

The next thing I knew, in mid-conversation, Elvis reached down between the cushion and the armrest I was sitting on and pulled out a .45 handgun. He shot the TV, not once but twice. *BANG! BANG!* I jumped up and away. My heartrate accelerated to about 200. I shouted, "What the hell!" I stared at Elvis in disbelief, my ears ringing. He casually put the gun back between the cushions and went back to eating his bacon and eggs. "That'll be enough of that shit," he said.

I went over to the phone and called the hotel manager. I told him who I was, and informed him that his TV had met with a violent death. I requested a new one. He didn't react in any way, which I thought was odd. He just said, "Okay." Within twenty minutes the old, dead TV with two bullet holes was hauled off to the TV graveyard, and a new one was installed in its place. Minutes later, Elvis looked at me and started laughing. I laughed right along with him. What else could I do?

The story behind Elvis's dislike of Robert Goulet had to do with something Robert said to Elvis on television. Robert, who didn't know Elvis personally, said, "Don't worry Elvis; I'll take care of all your girlfriends when you're gone." It had to do with Elvis leaving town and his screaming fans staying behind. Elvis was a little bit touchy about the remark and shouldn't have let it bother him, but it did. Elvis wasn't too fond of many singers, in general, but disliked Robert Goulet passionately.

On another occasion, when we were on tour somewhere, several of us were standing in Elvis's room getting ready to leave. Another innocent TV was quietly minding its own business, showing whatever was on at the time, when suddenly good ole Wild Bill Elvis hauled out his trusty .22 and fired a round at the poor hapless TV. This time the TV didn't break, probably because it was just a .22 instead of a .45, like the first incident. This time, the bullet ricocheted off the TV and hit Elvis's father, Vernon, in the chest. Vernon wasn't hurt. He just had a small mark on his chest.

I was glad I didn't have to report another dead TV to the hotel's management. I was quietly astounded that nobody seemed bothered at what had just taken place. Not even Vernon. He just brushed it off like the bullet he'd just brushed off his chest. We all quietly left the room and went on to the gig as if nothing happened.

ONE MORE EXCITING SHOOTOUT AT THE O.K. CORRAL: One time we were pulling into Graceland in a car that had a moon roof. Cars were parked on either side of the gate. One had a soda can on its roof. I noticed it right away, since I was driving. I thought *Oh no*! By that point I knew Elvis and his gun-slinging ways. Sure enough, the moon roof opened, Elvis stood up, took aim, and fired off a round at the evil, offensive can. He missed and the round went God-only-knows-where. The gate opened. I drove onto the grounds before Elvis could fire another round at that demonic can of soda.

Once again, I was astounded. There were people all around, as always, trying to get a glimpse of Elvis, and nobody noticed? Elvis just sat back down like it was nothing. All of us laughed like a bunch of chumps. Nobody ever made any kind of big deal about it, and there never were any repercussions.

THE KID WITH THE WATCHES: One day, while Elvis was appearing at the Hilton in Las Vegas, he decided to go to a gun store to buy some guns. Elvis, Red, Sonny, and I piled into a car and went to a gun store to check out the merchandise. What we failed to notice was that a member of the paparazzi had followed us to the gun store. He came in behind us, unnoticed. It was unusual for us to not notice one of those vampires, but on this occasion, we messed up.

We all just wandered around inside the store while Elvis looked at the weapons. After twenty minutes or so, Elvis started purchasing handguns. He even bought me a Colt Python, which I had for many years. As Elvis was paying for the guns, the photographer—who had been taking pics both outside and inside the store—got too close and we spotted him. We confronted the guy, without laying a hand on him, but he was belligerent. Elvis motioned to Red, Sonny, and me to hold off on the guy while he talked with him.

Elvis told the guy he didn't want pictures of himself purchasing guns published (they would've been sensational, to say the least). Elvis offered to pose for any pictures he wanted to take if he would agree to not publish the gun pictures. The guy knew he could make a small fortune selling the pictures to publications like the *Enquirer*. He mouthed off to Elvis, refusing his proposal.

As the bodyguards, we geared up to take the guy's camera away from him and expose the film when Elvis again told us to stand back. We all left. Later that evening, I learned that Elvis had made some phone calls. The result was that the pictures were confiscated, and the photographer was blacklisted. That shows the kind of power Elvis had.

All the guns Elvis purchased that day were in Sonny's name. Three days later, Elvis, Sonny, and I went back to the gun store to pick them up. There was a three-day waiting period for gun purchases. This time, however, Elvis drove the car while Sonny and I kept an eye out. When we got to the parking lot, Elvis and I stayed in the car while Sonny went in to pick up the guns.

The next thing we knew, there was this little kid outside the car. He was eleven years old. He looked at Elvis and said, "Hey Elvis wanna buy a watch?" Elvis looked over at me and laughed. He asked the kid how much the watches were. The kid told him, "Twenty bucks." Elvis looked at me with a grin and told me, "Give me a $100 bill." After I handed it to Elvis, he pulled out a pen and signed it before giving the money to the kid. Elvis then strapped on his crappy watch. Sonny came out with the purchases. The kid took off with his $100 bill wearing a big smile. We drove back to the Hilton.

The penthouse at the Hilton had three bedrooms, a large living room with a bar, and a kitchen. The main door, near the elevators, was manned by a security guard. It also had a service elevator behind the kitchen that chimed when it arrived at the penthouse. Sitting in the living room with Elvis the next day, I heard the service elevator chime. When I opened the door to see who was there, the kid with the watches from the day before was grinned out at me.

"Okay, you little stinker, what do you want now?" I asked. He was not intimidated in the slightest. He said, "I thought Elvis would want to buy some more watches." I really liked this little con man, so I told him, "Come with me." I brought him into the penthouse, and took him over to Elvis, who took one look at the kid and started laughing. He said exactly what I had. "What do you want now?"

The kid repeated what he had said to me. Elvis asked the kid how many watches he had on him. He had four crummy watches, and Elvis took all of them for $500.

I escorted the kid out to the front elevator telling him, "You did an excellent job, kid. But don't come back." He said, "Okay," and left. This little guy, all by himself, got past all the security and figured out how to get to the penthouse. I couldn't believe it. I'm sure he went on to become a millionaire.

Chapter 5: The Crazy Ladies

THE MAIL ORDER BRIDES: I was driving to Graceland one day for another fun day at work. As I got close, a television truck was driving away from the front gate. People were milling around outside around the gate, which caught my attention. I asked Vester, the gate guard, "What's going on with all the commotion?"

"See those two girls standing over there?" He pointed to our right.

"Yeah," I said, and looked at two young girls about ten feet away.

"They mailed themselves to Elvis."

"What?"

"Yeah, they mailed themselves to Elvis in a box."

I couldn't believe it. I had never heard of such a thing. I realized how much Elvis rubbed off on his fans, but to mail yourself to him in a box was just over the top. How the hell could a person even do that? I had to talk to them.

"Come here, ladies." I waved them over. They were only 17 or 18 years old. They walked over, looking nervous, and said, "Hello." They both looked down, like they knew they were going to get yelled at.

"Did you guys seriously do that? Put yourselves in a box and mail yourselves here to Elvis?" They shyly told me that they did. I asked them why in the world would in the world would they do that. They told me, "We were desperate to meet Elvis. We couldn't think of any other way."

"So, let me get this straight," I said, still dumbfounded. "You put yourselves in a box, with air holes in it, I assume, and then had someone mail you here?" They confirmed, so I asked them how they thought they could mail two people in a box.

"We identified the contents of the box as a dog."

"How much did it cost for postage?" I asked.

"Ninety seven dollars," they replied/

"Obviously it worked. So, what happened when the box arrived here?" They told me that the box was delivered to the office in a small building in the back of Graceland, but the office personnel refused to accept delivery. "We don't want a dog." When the girls heard that, they kicked their way out of the box. They were caught. Shortly after, someone called a local television station, which sent a truck out to cover the event.

I admired those two young ladies for their courage and sheer inventiveness to pull off such an outrageous stunt, only to fail at meeting their goal at the last second. I was so impressed that I asked them, "You still want to meet Elvis?" Of course, they did. I told them to get into the car, and I drove them to the back of Graceland, where I normally parked.

I took them inside. As we walked down the hallway I saw Elvis in the jungle room watching TV.

"Hey Elvis," I said, "Guess what I got here!"

"Two pretty girls?" he responded.

"Yep, you're not going to believe what these two pretty girls just did."

"What?"

"They put themselves in a box and mailed themselves to you."

Elvis couldn't believe it. He asked them why they would do such a thing. "We wanted to meet you," one of the girls said.

Elvis looked at me in disbelief and laughed. "Well, it worked," he said. "You got to meet me." They chatted for a while then Elvis shot me a look. It was time for the girls to go. I told them it was time to head out, explaining to never do anything that crazy again.

I hope they're alive and well. I wonder what they're telling their grandchildren about their Elvis adventure.

THE HIGH DIVER: At the Omni in Atlanta the stage was 15-20 feet high. It backed up to within three or four feet of a balcony a few feet above us.

During every show, Elvis visited each part of the stage, singing to as many people in the audience as possible. He would sing to the group in front of him, giving out scarves.

At one point during this concert, Elvis went to the back of the stage to sing to the folks in the balcony. Because of the height of the stage and the spotlights shining in Elvis's eyes, he couldn't see the gap between the stage and the balcony, so I went with him. I knelt and placed my hand on Elvis's knee so he would know not to go any closer to the edge of the stage.

Elvis sang for a while, threw some scarves into the balcony, turned around, and started to walk away. At that moment, a girl rushed to the edge of the balcony. The rail around the balcony was only three feet tall. I realized the girl wasn't going to stop. Sure enough, she launched herself over the balcony like a high diver in the Olympics. Instinctively, I reached out and caught her in midair, if you consider the both of us crashing to the edge of the stage "catching" her.

Directly, this girl slipped over the edge of the stage with me holding onto her for dear life. Luckily, a few of the security guys saw what was happening and rushed over to help get her down safely.

"Are you crazy?" I asked sternly. "Why did you do that? You could have killed yourself and me along with you."

"I wanted a scarf," she replied.

I had the guards hold her while I went and got her a scarf. Then I told them to remove her from the premises. I couldn't believe it, all for a scarf, seriously?

The things women did in Elvis's presence were unbelievable.

FUN WITH THE CURTAIN: We occupied the Las Vegas Hilton quite often. The stage at the Hilton was curved out toward the audience in the center and bowed back on the sides. The curtain opened and closed in a straight line from side to side. As an aside, Elvis never did encores. The audience thought if they just clapped hard enough and yelled loud enough for a long enough period of time, he would come back out and sing a few more. They were wrong. It's just something Elvis never did. He wanted to escape as quickly as possible, usually to a limo waiting for him in a secluded area outside.

While the fans tried to get an encore, we used that time as a window of opportunity to get out of the venue before the crowd could descend on us. As we were leaving, we often heard the now famous words, "Elvis has left the building." At the Hilton, however, he didn't leave the building. Instead, we went to the dressing room and then to the penthouse to have a little fun ourselves. At the end of the show, what happened was Elvis would sing his last song and the curtains would close. We would then open the curtains wide enough for Elvis to stand with his hands raised in the form of a V (sort of like President Nixon's "I am not a crook" stance).

The problem was that we couldn't see the edge of the stage, and we couldn't see anyone coming at Elvis from the side. Sonny—Mr. Brilliant Idea—said to me, "You know, Dave, if you push the edge of the curtain out to the edge of the stage, nobody can get by from the side."

"That's a great idea, Sonny," I said. "I'm going to do that."

Elvis was finishing the show and did a bunch of his fancy moves to keep the crowd cheering, and did his bows with the music at the end as I pushed the curtain to the edge of the stage, and it worked—for a minute. The next thing I knew, a pair of hands grabbed my leg from under the curtain. Then another pair of hands grabbed my other leg, pulling me down and under the curtain. I looked over to Sonny, Red, and Elvis and yelled, "Help! Hey! You guys, help!" The curtain was now closed.

The guys just looked at me as these women dragged me under the curtain, laughed, and despite my pleas for help, walked away. "Have a wonderful time, Dave."

These crazy women dragged me down under the curtain and onto their table, as drinks flew everywhere. One of them said, "Gotcha." Resigned to my fate, I said, "Okay," and had an exciting time with the ladies. It was a difficult job, but somebody had to do it. I was just looking out for Elvis.

If keeping those beautiful women company was what Elvis wanted, that's what I had to do. What a time it was.

GUNS CAN BE A LIABILITY: The story behind the first female I ever stopped from getting to Elvis was an interesting and unforgettable experience. We were at the Sahara Tahoe. Before the show, Elvis had given me a .38 handgun, but he didn't give me a holster. I just put the gun down the front of my pants, gangster style, often referred to as 'appendix carry' and covered it up with my jacket. I didn't think much about it then, but had that puppy gone off I'd be missing some manhood.

Once the show was in progress, I was standing by the curtain scanning the crowd, when I noticed this morbidly obese woman waddling quickly toward the stage. She jumped up on the table, which was quite impressive for a big woman, especially since there was no springboard, and ran awkwardly toward the stage. By the time she hit the stage, she had a full head of steam; she was motoring faster than I'd ever seen anybody that huge run.

I knew I had to stop her, so I jumped in front of her. She kept running right through me. Unfortunately for me, she crashed into the gun, which slammed into my abdomen. It felt like it went through my back. She busted me up pretty good. I had a nasty bruise on my stomach for a week. She was so focused on getting to Elvis that I don't think she even saw me in front of her.

During that incident, I thought, *Oh Lord, I hope it's not all going to be like this.* It wasn't, of course, but what could I do? I couldn't hurt them. I had to be as gentle as possible, so if anybody was going to get hurt, it was going to be me. I did manage to stop the woman, however. Elvis came over, laughing, and gave her a scarf. It probably didn't fit her. I mean, her neck was the size of an average woman's waist.

I had many learning experiences as a bodyguard and that was one of them. Don't conceal a pistol without a holster; screw the 'appendix carry.' I never made that mistake again.

GUYS ON STAGE: We didn't worry too much when girls got on stage. We always knew why they were jumping up there, but when a guy jumped on the stage, we were keyed up for anything. What's a guy doing on the stage? That could be real trouble. The way we worked it was, Sonny and I would be on one side of the stage, and Red and Dick would be on the other side. Off the stage, directly in front and to the sides, would be additional security officers who were responsible for anything off the stage. We four were responsible for anything on the stage.

Sonny and I would look to the other side of the stage beyond Red and Dick's curtain, and they would look to our side of the stage beyond our curtain. So, if I saw someone coming on the stage on Red and Dick's side, I signaled them and they went into action. Same thing if they saw someone beyond our curtain. It worked well, except for this one occasion.

I saw a girl jump up onto the stage on Red and Dick's side when she bolted toward Elvis. When I gave Red the signal, he came out around the curtain and grabbed her before she could get to Elvis. Then a guy jumped onto the stage. Red was occupied with taking care of the girl and didn't see him. I took off after the guy, scooped him up, and slammed him to the stage floor. Then I bent him over my knee. I heard him yelling, but couldn't understand what he was saying. Then I finally got it.

"I'm security!" He was a new security guard; this was his first day on the job. He thought *he* was supposed to catch the girl. He didn't realize he wasn't supposed to get on stage. Unfortunately, during the scuffle, I tore up his brand-new suit jacket and ripped his patent leather shoe, and embarrassed him beyond belief.

After the show, I went to the new guy's boss and asked him to not reprimand the guy. He was just trying to do his job. I also asked his boss to apologize to the guy for me because I didn't realize he was security. Lastly, I told the guy's boss to buy the guy a new pair of shoes and a new suit.

Chapter 6: Random Stories

RECORDING AT GRACELAND: We finished a concert in Shreveport, LA, and went back to the hotel trying to unwind. Lamar Fike, Felton Jarvis, and I went off to the hotel lounge where we got a table, ordered a few drinks, and kicked back to watch and listen to the lounge act. The duo consisted of a guy playing keyboard and a girl on guitar. She was also the lead vocalist. The girl was extremely attractive, and she had an amazing voice. After a few songs, I mentioned to the guys how impressed I was with this girl's voice. Felton Jarvis was Elvis's record producer for RCA, and the funniest human I had ever met.

Both Lamar and Felton agreed with my assessment of the girl's amazing talent. We were enjoying listening to her when she announced the last song. She thanked everyone for listening and being a great audience, and then she went on to sing her final song for the night. We wanted to hear more, so Felton said, "Dave, when they're done with this last song, go on over there and see if you can talk them into doing another set."

I walked over, introduced myself, complimented them on their performance, and asked if they'd be willing to do another set. They both said things like, "Thank you, but it's too late." "It's been a long night." . . . and, "We're tired." They quickly changed their minds when I started peeling off $100 bills. They did another set, made a nice chunk of change, and we enjoyed the rest of the show.

During their final set, after another round of drinks arrived, I said to Felton, "Felton, that girl has an amazing voice. You should sign her up."

"Dave, it's the song," he replied.

"But Felton, you have to admit she has an incredible voice."

"Dave, you don't understand. Sure, she has a great voice, but there are thousands of female singers just like her. It's the song, Dave." I didn't want to give up, so I pushed a little harder until he finally said, "Dave, relax! I'm going to talk to her, but you just have to understand that it's not her or her great voice, it's the song."

Months later, we were at Graceland where Elvis was doing some recording. The jungle room at Graceland had the walls covered in carpet, which made it suitable for recording. In the room with me was the band and Felton Jarvis, while a few technicians occupied an RCA recording truck outside. We were hanging out waiting for Elvis to come down, when Felton said over the intercom, "Hey Dave, we're doing a sound check. Do you know any Elvis songs?" I told him I did. He said, "Go ahead and sing a few bars."

At that point, I realized that Felton was setting me up somehow and I told him, "You know damn well I have an awful singing voice. You're just trying to embarrass me." He insisted that he just needed a sound check of someone singing. I still didn't believe him, but the guys in the band told me to go ahead and do it. They would accompany me. Reluctantly, I agreed.

The recording started, the band began playing, and I started singing. I got through only a few bars. That was enough for me; I stopped singing. Felton said over the intercom, "Thanks Dave. Now hold on a minute." After a couple moments, he came back on. "Okay, Dave, this is what you sound like," and he played the recording. I sounded like I had been lit on fire. Felton said, "Hang on a minute." Then he came back. "Listen now." To my utter amazement, I sounded great. I couldn't believe how good I sounded. The guys in the band were all clapping and smiling. Felton had adjusted the levels of my wretched voice by lowering the highs and elevating the lows. He probably added in a bunch of voodoo, because nothing short of magic could fix my horrible singing voice. As I stood there wondering how he made me sound so good, Felton once again came over the intercom and said, "It's the song, Dave." He got his point across.

PARTING THE CLOUD: Like the other guys, I indulged Elvis to no end, but I was always battling with my laugh button, especially when he went into his "mystical power" and "psychic healing skills." I vividly recall one instance when we were at his Palm Springs house. It was hotter than hell ever was—110° at least. Elvis wanted me to drive him to the mall to load up on groceries and whatever else any of us wanted. I got in the driver's seat and Elvis was riding shotgun. A couple of the other guys decided to go with us, so they hopped in the back.

As sweltering as it was, it was a gorgeous day. Naturally, we had the air conditioning on. We made it to the mall and Elvis bought just about everything in sight. We loaded the vehicle up with his purchases, and I drove back toward the house.

The sky was completely clear, blue as ever, except for one tiny cloud. It was up there minding its own business. Nobody even noticed it until Elvis demanded, "Stop the car!" I slammed on the brake. As I looked over wondering what was going on, he said, "Turn off the engine."

I thought something might be wrong with the car. I hadn't noticed anything. I turned the vehicle off and asked him, "What's going on?" Because the AC wasn't running, the interior temperature rose to at least 180°. I felt like I was going to pass out. We all were instantly drenched in sweat and gasping for air. Elvis ordered, "Be quiet while I concentrate." As I was wondering what he was doing, he said, "See that cloud over there?" I looked up to see the little, lonesome cloud. We all looked and told him that we saw it. It was the only cloud in the sky.

Elvis started talking about the power of metaphysics and how, through years of study, he had *the power* in abundance. "Watch this," he said. He stared at the cloud. The rest of us looked at each other like he was nuts. He told us he was going to make the cloud disappear using the power of his mind.

Sweating profusely, I thought to myself, *Come on, cloud. Move. Do something, for God's sake.* We were dying in that car. Not a sound could be made in that oven of a car while Elvis was wielding his *awesome power.* At the same time, I was having a problem holding back from bursting out laughing. I didn't though; I knew Elvis would be mortally insulted and hurt.

We were there for what seemed like an hour . . . but it was only ten minutes or so. Finally, that little cloud moved slightly and dissipated a bit. As you probably know, if you watch a cloud, any cloud, for any length of time, it will move and/or change appearance—even slightly dissipating at times. I take credit for saving the day. I noticed it first, and because I didn't want to die of dehydration or heat stroke, I said, "Hey, it moved!" That turned out to be the right thing to say. Elvis looked at me with one of those sly little smiles that told me he had done it again. "I know," he said. "I moved it." I immediately fired up the engine, cranked up the air conditioner, and drove us back to the house. Mission accomplished.

THE INFAMOUS SANDWICH: Elvis ate some of the most horrible stuff you would ever want to eat, and he loved every second of it. One of those gems was his famous peanut butter and banana sandwich, fried in butter. One day, Elvis and I were in his room bullshitting and he was eating this sandwich that, at first glance, looked like grilled cheese.

As Elvis chowed down on that sandwich, I noticed that the cheese was brown. *What the hell kind of cheese is brown?* I thought. Initially, I thought it was viciously overcooked, but there's no way that would be tasty. Judging by the way Elvis was downing that sandwich, like it was the only thing that existed in his world at that moment, he was enjoying it immensely. My curiosity got the best of me, so I asked, "What are you eating?"

He told me, "Peanut butter and banana sandwich, fried in butter. It's delicious. You should go down to the kitchen and ask Mary to make you one."

Since I liked peanut butter, and I liked bananas, it sounded good. I thought I'd give it a try. I went down to the kitchen and asked Mary to make me one. She pulled out a frying pan and tossed a whole stick of butter—*quarter pound* of butter (!) in the pan. While it was melting, she took a piece of bread and slapped on about a half-an-inch layer of peanut butter, sliced up a banana and put it on there, and put the other piece of bread on top. By that time the butter in the pan had melted, so she plopped the sandwich in the pan for 15 seconds, then turned it over to soak up the remaining butter, and fried the sandwich.

I couldn't believe the amount of butter she used to make that sandwich. She handed it to me. I took two bites and began to gag. It was so rich. I couldn't handle it. There were times when Elvis would eat six of them in one sitting.

From that point on I couldn't even watch Elvis eat one without gagging. Boy, did he love that sandwich.

ELVIS THE GIVER: Elvis was the most generous person I have ever met. He bought cars, motorcycles, trucks, clothing, jewelry, and gave money to not only his friends and family, but also to complete strangers. He always did it with a good heart. To give you an idea of what it was like to be on the receiving end of his generosity, I'll tell you the story of the car, which is one of many.

We were driving down the street in Memphis, TN. I don't remember who was driving, but Elvis was in the front passenger seat and I was in the back. We were just driving around shooting the shit. The three of us were telling stories, joking and laughing. We were having a wonderful time enjoying each other's company. Suddenly, on a whim, Elvis said, "Hey, Dave."

"What?" I asked.

"I want to buy you a car."

"Elvis, you just gave me a Mercedes a year-and-a-half ago. You don't have to buy me another car."

"I know I don't have to buy you another car, but I *want* to buy you another car."

"That's very nice of you, but don't feel as though you need to, or anything."

The next thing I knew, he turned around and a loaded gun was pointing in my face. "You're gonna take this fucking car or I'm gonna blow your fucking head off."

"Okay," I said. "I didn't think you were serious, Elvis." I knew he loved to give glamorous gifts to just about anybody, but I didn't want him to feel like I was using him for gifts. I quickly learned: If he wants to gift me something, just be grateful and thank him. Don't make him uncomfortable by telling him it isn't necessary. Of course, I loved everything he gave me and appreciated his kindness.

The car was a 1974 Lincoln Continental Mark Four. Elvis bought eight of us cars that day. Two of us got Lincolns and everybody else got Cadillacs. Elvis gave us a choice and that's what we chose. Lamar Fike was the other guy who got a Lincoln. Lamar's car had all the bells and whistles—the extras, like a moon roof, among other cool things. Mine was just a plain Lincoln . . . not that there was anything wrong with a brand new plain Lincoln—especially a free one. It just didn't have any of the goodies. It was still a beautiful car.

Lamar busted my balls a bit saying his Lincoln was better than mine. Then, for some reason I'm not aware of, Elvis got pissed off at the dealers where he got all our cars. This was a couple days later. Suddenly Elvis said, "We're going back to the dealers and giving them back the goddamn cars." There we were with brand new cars we had been driving for a couple days, and we had to take them back. We took them back to the dealers and left.

The next day, Elvis told me that he was still going to get me a car, but it would be from a different dealer. I told him I appreciated his kindness and said I'd like another Lincoln. He told me, "You can have whatever you want." He said to call a specific dealer and get it ordered. He would take care of it.

I called up a Lincoln dealership, got a hold of the head guy, told him who I was, and that Elvis was going to buy me a Lincoln. I described the exact Lincoln I was looking for—the kind Lamar had had, with all the fixings. The guy told me he had that exact car, and he would deliver it to Graceland for me. Once my new Lincoln with all the extras was parked there, everybody was admiring it. Lamar walked out, took one look at it and said, "You sonofabitch." He recognized that my new car was his former car that he was busting my chops over. Of course, I deliberately told the dealer to give me the exact car that was originally given to Lamar

For some reason, Vernon had my car registered in Elvis's name. Elvis found out a day or two later and told Vernon he didn't want the car registered in his name. He wanted it in my name, since it was my car. The original paperwork said it was sold to Elvis Presley, but he wanted it to say the buyer was Dave Hebler. Any time Elvis bought someone a car, and there were many times, he always had the vehicle put in that person's name. It was just a slip-up on Vernon's part.

I was driving the car home to California, with the original paperwork and change of title in hand. As I drove through Oklahoma City, I got pulled over by a highway patrolman. He ran my plate and noticed that it belonged to Elvis Presley. He thought I stole the car from Elvis. I told him I worked for Elvis and that he had bought me the car. I explained that once I got to California, where I lived, I would register the car in my name.

The patrolman told me that he had no way of verifying if what I told him was true. I asked him if he knew a sergeant at the Oklahoma City Police Department by the name of Sugar Smith. He did, so I told him to give Sugar a call and he would tell him that what I was saying was true. Sure enough, he called Sugar and it was verified. The patrolman wished me well and I continued on home. Once I arrived, I registered the vehicle in my name. I drove that car for 20 years and put a quarter of a million miles on it. I ended up selling it to a guy who had the Elvis-A-Rama Museum in Las Vegas, Nevada.

When I sold the car, it was sitting in a storage yard because I had blown the water pump. I had another car, so I had just put this one in storage. The guy from the museum bought the car, along with some of my other stuff. He was the editor of *Hot Boat* magazine, so he had access to all kinds of mechanics who worked on engines and did bodywork. He was in the process of refurbishing the car and fixing the engine. They did the job, fired up the engine, and unfortunately, the car caught on fire in the process. They put the fire out, but the vehicle had severe damage.

The guy I sold it to told me he spent close to $25,000 rebuilding the car. The original color was silver. He hated silver-colored cars, and knew my favorite color was purple, so he painted it purple. The car originally had a red velour interior, which he thought was tacky, so he replaced that with white leather and purple piping. Today that car sits on display at Graceland.

I'll give you another example of Elvis's generosity. One day I said to him, "Elvis, do you have any idea how many cars and motorcycles you've given away in the last two years?"

"No, and I don't care," he responded. "Wait a minute!" he added. "I want to show you something." He left the room for a moment and came back with a $100,000 check made out to him. It was one of many that'd come before, and many more after. "You know, I know that I cannot buy the goodwill that comes when I buy somebody a car. The publicity and the goodwill I get cannot be bought. And this check, it seems like every time I do something nice for someone, it comes back to me a hundred times over. Besides, it makes me feel good to make people happy."

That was the generous side of Elvis Presley.

Image Section

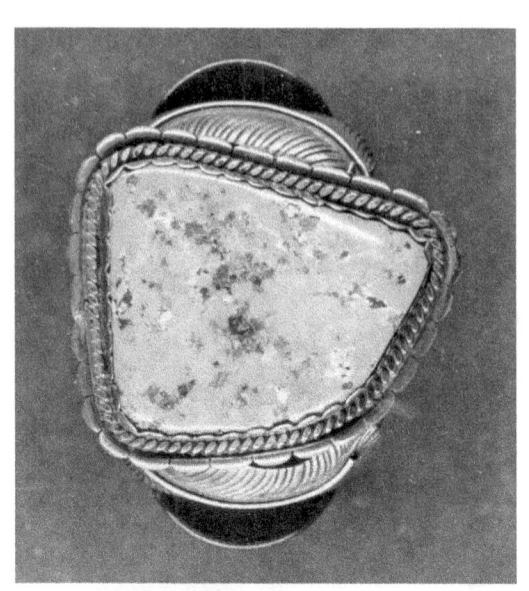

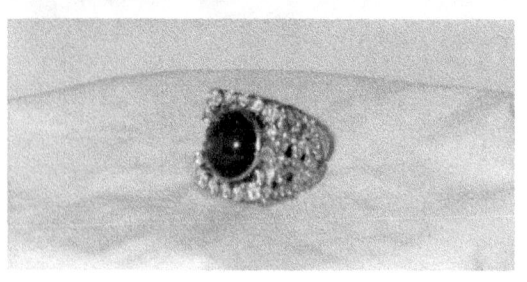

Chapter 7: Playing with the Colonel

During the time I worked for Elvis, I had more than a few interactions with the Colonel—Elvis's manager. I understand that the Colonel is widely reviled by most everyone in the Elvis community, and perhaps with good reason, but my experiences with him will possibly show another side of this man.

Prior to 1972, and continuing for many years, I had no idea about the Colonel and his history. It just never came up, and I really wasn't interested in finding out. So, with the certain knowledge that I could not write this book without including a chapter on the Colonel, here it is:

ANOTHER SIDE TO THE COLONEL: The Colonel liked to play; especially with me, and when I say "play," I really mean the Colonel tried to put me in awkward situations to see if he could put one over on me. Every time he tried, he lost. I loved outsmarting the big bad Colonel. He was always a good sport. He just tried harder the next time. Here are a few stories with the Colonel to prove my point.

THE $100 CHIP: As many people already know, the Colonel had a major gambling problem. So, it wasn't unusual for him to be walking around with $100 chips in his pockets in Las Vegas. One day, in the public area of the dressing room at the Hilton in Las Vegas, the Colonel stood next to Elvis holding a $100 chip between his thumb and forefinger when he said, "Hey Dave, see this chip?" I was only about six feet away from him and told him, "I can see it clearly."

"If you can take this chip out of my fingers before Elvis can, it's yours," he said.

I shot forward, snatched the chip out of his fingers, and said, "Gee thanks, Colonel."

"Wait," he said, "You cheated. Give that chip back." I gave him his chip back. He wanted a second go-around. This time, however, he placed the chip in the palm of his hand and said, "Okay, let's try this again."

Once again, I shot forward. This time I slapped the back of his hand so that the chip flew up in the air. I then dove down and caught the chip before it hit the floor, smiled up at the Colonel, and then handed him the chip. The look on his face was as if he had just seen a ghost. Elvis just laughed. The Colonel thought he could outsmart me, that I wouldn't be fast enough to get the chip from him. He never did give me that chip, even though I took it from him twice. The bragging rights were good enough for me, however.

THE CHAIR: On another trip to Las Vegas, and in the same dressing room, the Colonel had another trick up his sleeve. The dressing room at the Hilton was two rooms: Elvis's private dressing room and another room for guests. This room had a bar with stools and several chairs where guests and the rest of us lounged around.

On this occasion, I was sitting on one of the bar stools and the Colonel was standing in front of me wiggling his fingers in my face, and saying, "You are hypnotized. You cannot do anything unless the Colonel says so. You cannot leave that chair unless the Colonel says you can."

And with that, the Colonel went into Elvis's dressing room. A minute or so later Elvis shouted, "Dave, come in here. I need to speak with you."

I thought for a moment. *Okay, now what, Coach?* As quick-witted as I am, I grabbed the top of the stool, held it tightly to my ass, stood up with it attached to me, and slowly walked into Elvis's room. I gracefully plopped myself down in Elvis's room, stool and all, and said, "Yeah, Elvis, what did you want to speak with me about?"

Once again Elvis just laughed, looked at the Colonel, and said, "He gotcha again, Colonel." The Colonel was dumbfounded. He tried repeatedly throughout my years with Elvis to get one up on me. He never succeeded, no matter how many times he attempted. I swear he would sit around for hours drawing up plans of action to finally get me with something. Nice try, Colonel. Eventually, he stopped trying.

THE WHEEL: The Colonel played roulette—probably the dumbest game to play in the pit. The odds are only marginally better than Keno. By the way, as a former pit boss and dealer for 15 years, I can tell you that there is no game in any casino in which the odds are in your favor, so don't go there expecting to win. Just have fun within your budget. If you happen to get lucky, have some more fun. I won't go into detail regarding the value of roulette chips, other than to say that they aren't worth anything until the player designates the value in real dollars.

When the Colonel played, his chips were worth $100 each and he bought them in every color. He stacked various chips on every bet possible, covering the layout with piles of chips of every color. This is known as "barber-poling."

Once again, we were hanging out in the dressing room, when the Colonel said to me, loud enough for the entire room to hear, "Hey Dave, I understand you lost a bunch of money today. How much did you lose?"

Thinking the Colonel was going to reimburse me, I said, "A thousand dollars, Colonel." Truthfully, I lost only $80.

"Let that be a lesson, Dave," the Colonel replied. "If you can't stand the heat, stay out of the kitchen." With that he walked away.

Later, I was walking through the casino and noticed the Colonel betting his brains out on the roulette wheel with stacks of various colored chips everywhere on the layout. It was roped off; he was the only player allowed in the game. Inside the ropes were two dealers, the pit boss, and a few security guards. Tom Hulett from Concerts West was also watching the action. As I walked by the table, the Colonel saw me, called me over and asked me to loan him $500. I didn't have that kind of money to loan him. I didn't know what to say.

As I tried to gather my thoughts, the pit boss saw me struggling and nodded to let me know that the $500 was on the house. The Colonel said, "Borrow it from Tom." Tom handed me the money, and I gave it to the Colonel. The Colonel turned it over to the dealer to change into roulette chips, which he liberally stacked on top of various bets.

The ball rolled, a number hit, the dealer cleared away the losing bets and paid the winning bets. The Colonel then gave a stack of roulette chips to the dealer telling him to change them up for real $100 chips, which turned out to be $1,500. The Colonel gave me the chips and told me to give Tom back his $500. Then he said, "That's your winnings Dave. Just remember, always stick with the Colonel." So, I received the $1000 that the Colonel thought I lost. It was a good day.

Chapter 8: Elvis and Gospel Music

Gospel deeply influenced Elvis throughout his life, and I find it fascinating to think about how he balanced it with life in show business as he constantly searched spiritually and intellectually. I recall that after concerts in Las Vegas and Lake Tahoe, where we spent weeks at a time, Elvis and most of his entourage gathered in Elvis's suite to sing gospel songs in fellowship with one another.

As I said earlier, I'm a terrible singer. When I sing, to say that it sounds like a bunch of cats dying a miserable death would be a compliment. God blessed me with some wonderful attributes, but singing wasn't one of them. Elvis, of course, noticed that immediately, just as everybody else did. He took delight in putting me in the spotlight to embarrass me and give himself and the rest of the crowd a good laugh. He did that often.

One time Elvis did that on stage, in the middle of a sold-out concert, in front of thousands of his fans. While he was singing, he never stayed in one spot. He wandered all over the stage to sing intimately to as many fans as possible. I didn't think it unusual when Elvis wandered over to my side of the stage, where I lurked behind the edge of the curtain. Suddenly, he grabbed the curtain and pulled it away, revealing me to the audience. He then stuck the microphone in my face. "Sing the song, Dave."

Damn, that was awkward. I didn't know what to do, so I uttered a few obscenities at him, amplified by the microphone. He busted up laughing, walked away, and resumed singing. Funny, though, he never did that to me again during a concert.

Although Elvis had a wonderful time messing with me and my awful singing voice, sitting around with everyone, singing songs with Elvis was a lot of fun. He got serious, however, when it came to gospel songs. Anytime a gospel song was being sung, he demanded silence from everyone who was not participating. He allowed me, with my terrible voice, to opt out during those times. He didn't want the Lord condemning me for such a terrible sin. Elvis joked about it, saying, "Every time you sing, Satan himself prays for you to stop." He said that if I ever encountered a demon, rather than rebuking him in the name of Jesus, all I'd have to do was sing. That demon would bolt out of there faster than hell (no pun intended) and never bother me again.

In the mid-1970s, Elvis did a gig at Oral Roberts University in Tulsa, OK, an interdenominational, Christian comprehensive liberal arts university. The concert went well. As we were leaving the concert hall, Elvis and the rest of us noticed flyers stuck to our vehicles. The flyers read *who's the real King?* And, *there is only one King.*

Elvis grabbed one of the flyers from the windshield and just shook his head, looking a little upset. "Why are they doing this?" he asked. "I never said I was the king of anything. Other people say that stuff. I have always said there's only one king, and that is Jesus Christ. I'm just a singer." He didn't say anything else, but it was apparent he was hurt by it. Just like he was hurt when preachers condemned him in his early career, declaring that he was singing the devil's music, and that the way he performed was disgusting and immoral.

Elvis never forgot how he was treated by those preachers in the early days of his career. He also never forgot about what happened a few years later. He became an overnight sensation and was a rich icon. All those same preachers contacted him wanting money, houses, and performances at their churches, gratis. Some of them even wanted him on their television shows. To his credit, Elvis never lost his faith in the gospel, or in gospel music, despite the horrible manner he was treated by preachers.

Throughout Elvis's life, he never strayed from his faith in Jesus Christ, despite indulging in the things that came with fame and often went against what he believed. Over and over he returned to his gospel roots, which brought him comfort and clarity, even in the fog. He read his Bible diligently, quoted scriptures often, and asked for God's forgiveness daily. Occasionally, I would see Elvis close his eyes, bow his head, and say a little prayer. He was never shy about displaying his faith. If anybody asked him anything regarding it, he'd sometimes talk for hours.

While writing this book, I came across an article on Elvis and gospel at www.musiclyric4christian.com which detailed the genesis of Elvis and gospel music in a way that spoke to me. It was written by Katherine Morey, owner of the site. I have her permission to include the article in this book. Here it is (as it is on the site - unedited):

ELVIS PRESLEY SANG GOSPEL

The fact that Elvis Presley sang gospel before he ever sang rock n roll might come as a surprise to some people. They might also be shocked to learn that this hip-swinging, guitar-playing King of Rock-n-Roll, first guitar was a gift from his Pentecostal pastor.

ELVIS PRESLEY SANG GOSPEL & HOW IT INFLUENCED HIS LIFE

"I ain't no saint," voiced Elvis Presley, "but I've tried on no account to do anything that would damage my relations or arouse God . . . I presume all any kid needs is love and the sense he or she belongs. If I could do or say anything that would grant some kid that perception, I would presume I had contributed something to the universe."

ELVIS PRESLEY SANG GOSPEL BACKGROUND

He was born and raised in the Gospel Zone of America, and his household attended the First Assembly of God Church whose Pentecostal services commonly included singing. "When Elvis Presley was only a little kid, he would glide off my lap, run down the aisle, and crawled up to the stage of the church. He would stand looking eagerly up at the choir and tried to sing with them," voiced his mum, Gladys.

In 1946, Elvis Presley asked his parents for a bicycle, but Gladys, being totally shielding of Elvis, was terrified that he might fall off and injure himself, and swerved Elvis to get a guitar instead. The following year, his papa Vernon's brother, Johnny Smith and Assembly of God Pastor Frank Smith, gave him fundamental guitar lessons. Soon he was listening to the radio, tuning into a range of music as he tried to select out melodies.

Elvis Presley Sang Gospel with the Big-Named Groups

In 1954 Elvis Presley went to the Mississippi-Alabama State Fair. It was there, at the age of ten, that Elvis stood on a bench in front of a large crowd, unescorted by music, and sang *Old Shep,* a warm-hearted ballad concerning a boy and his dog. To his delight he was awarded 2nd Prize for the very 1st time for singing. Elvis experienced a basic but significant tip that day. His utterance was resilient and singing could produce his fantasies to become a reality.

In his consecutive youth, Elvis Presley could be seen at every gospel performance appearing in Memphis. It was during this period that he was befriended by such gospel greats as J. D. Sumner and the Blackwood Brothers, as well as numerous of the Black gospel groups. He was frequently invited backstage and would connect with them in melody.

Because of this force, he ripened into a unique style that incorporated the styles of all of these groups. His favorite singer at this time was Jake Hess. Jake is still on the move in gospel music via the concerts organized by the Gaither Reunion. Elvis won the older ability competition at Humes High School just before his 1953 graduation.

His First Recording

On completion of his graduation he took a job at Parker Machinists Store. By June was employed at the Precision Tool Company and hitherto drove heavy vehicles for the Crown Electric Company. He was seen most of this time on Beale Street and frequented the all-night white and black "Gospel Chorus" that were held downtown.

On the way out to jobs in a Ford pick-up, Elvis would make his way by the Memphis Recording Service. One Saturday, Elvis Presley stopped by the recording services with his old guitar and recorded his mum a birthday gift. Elvis cut 2 songs, *My Happiness*, and the 2nd, *That's When Your Heartaches Start*.

Resulting, the tape was given to the manager, Sam C. Phillips, proprietor of Sun Records and Elvis was invited to tape varied competent records. Rock and roll history was made when Elvis Presley, Scotty Moore, and Bill Black performed bluesman Arthur "Big Boy" Cruddup's *That's All Right* in a light-hearted, up-pulse fashion.

Elvis' First Public Official Performance

Elvis made his first official stage presence at Overton Park Shell in Memphis. Elvis was extremely apprehensive as he walked out to perform *Good Rockin' Tonight*. He felt his voice wasn't doing it unescorted, so he threw his body into the music, his feet began to shuffle, the knees bowed and shook, his hips swiveled and pumped in interval to the music.

"The first time that I appeared on stage, it terrified me to death. I genuinely didn't grasp what all the yelling was about. I didn't realize that my body was moving. It's a natural thing to me. So to the proprietor backstage I voiced, 'What'd I do? What'd I do?' And he uttered 'Whatever it is, go back and do it again'."

Elvis Presley Sang Gospel With Natural Ability

From a 1972 taped conversation used in MGM's documentary *Elvis on Tour*. Elvis was blessed with a natural ability to sing just about anything, but he needed to sense as tranquil with his picked-out material, as he was around the guys that worked for him. Elvis had a tenor utterance and a solid 3-octave scope. He loved to sing the bass parts, but he could hit the lofty notes so distinctly and dramatically that it came to be certified as one of the pre-eminent aspects of his style.

Elvis sought a personal "grasp" in all things that he did; which might develop from the pattern of the music, but most of the time it was more likely to come from something in the lyric, which would allow him to communicate himself.

Elvis Presley Sang Gospel - The Performance

Senior fans recall watching him perform his gospel performance of *Peace in the Valley* on the Ed Sullivan Show. This performance proved to numerous skeptical parents and righteous critics uniformly that he was not only a "hip-shaking rock and roller." It demonstrated that his understanding and conveyance of gospel music was rare, and was based on childhood and teen years of presence and singing alongside his mum at church and tent revivals.

He knew and could sing from recollection a large number of gospel and hymnal songs. Elvis once voiced "I know almost every god-fearing melody that's been written."

Predominantly, Elvis took gratification in listening to gospel. Elvis passionately believed that there was nothing as powerful or touching as the commendable gospel music. When traveling he would carry around a case of a hundred or so albums—most of them were gospel music.

Listening to his preferred gospel music was a means for Elvis to get in touch with his bloodline; he frequently used this music for giving praise to the Lord when feeling modest and grateful, which he constantly did. The word of God says to sing praise and lift your voice to Him.

Elvis wasn't one to sing a melody unless he felt it; he had to feel it in his heart, for that's where he sang from, and that's what made him a renowned star. No matter what he sang it had to fit him completely, and it is clear when going through songs he sang over the years, and hearing the personal connections that were evident in his life. When Elvis sang *How Great Thou Art* he felt it in his being, with such sensitivity and meaning he had the power in him to move mountains.

Elvis Presley Sang Gospel with Perseverance

A Marty Robbins's hit, *You Gave Me a Mountain* articulated his need to persevere, stay sturdy, carry on with strength after his break-up, and the despondency of being without his daughter. *American Trilogy*, one Elvis put together, as an honor to the stateliness of his nation and its custom. Only Elvis could have pulled it off with such perfection. "There is something spellbound about watching a man who has lost himself discover his way back home . . . . He sang with the kind of power people no longer envisage." - John Landau Review of *Elvis* (1968 TV Special).

ELVIS PRESLEY SANG GOSPEL - HIS FAVORITE MUSIC

There is no question Elvis Presley's favorite music was Gospel. He warmed up for story sessions with gospel songs, and when not on tour was repeatedly at his residence piano knocking out his favorite hymns. Elvis quite often sought after to listen to Mahalia Jackson, the Queen of Gospel.

Elvis Presley only scored one big gospel hit on the pop charts during his extraordinary profession - 1965's *Crying In The Chapel*, a re-release of a performance from 1960, coming at a period when he desperately required it, but gospel music, both "white" and "black," was a significant component of both his singing style and his worldview.

During his celebrated career it was Gospel, and Gospel music alone, that earned him the coveted Grammy awards - 1967 winner Best Sacred Performance for his *How Great Thou Art* album.

In the 1970s, Elvis Presley sang gospel songs more and more in his concerts and had the "Imperials" and the "Sweet Inspirations," as well as "JD Sumner & the Stamps," as his gospel backing group singers. Elvis also sometimes read passages from the Bible on stage during his concerts and insisted that audiences were respectfully quiet while *Sweet, Sweet Spirit* was sung by his backup group.

The gospel song *Life* was recorded by Elvis in 1970. In the year 2000 it was also included on the 3-CD set, *Elvis - Peace in the Valley- the Complete Gospel Recordings*. *Lead Me, Guide Me i*s one of Elvis' most touching performances from 1971 and when he sings, "I am lost if you take your hand from me," he seems so totally sincere it is truly moving.

In 1972, the gospel album *He Touched Me* is released to favorable reviews, and wins Elvis his 2nd Grammy Award. Elvis's live recording of *How Great Thou Art* in 1975 receives the Grammy Award for Best Inspirational Performance.

Elvis Presley Sang Gospel From the Heart

His gospel music is much loved by Elvis fans worldwide. Elvis read his Bible and prayed constantly and was very up to date about spiritual matters. In the mid-1960's he also held Bible studies in his Bel Air home where he lived while making his movies. He at no time sought after being called "The King". When an adoring fan called him the King one day, Elvis replied to her "No Honey, there is only one King and that is Jesus Christ."

June 26, 1977, Elvis gave his concluding performance in Madison Square Arena at Indianapolis, Indiana. It was in some of these latter performances, when Elvis Presley sang gospel that one could see the power he felt and emitted while singing gospel, spiritual and inspirational songs mixed in with his "rock" numbers. "Until we meet you again, may God bless you. Adios." - Elvis uttered in 1977 at the end of a performance during his final tour.

August 6, Elvis Presley sang gospel and hymns such as *How Great Thou Art* with companions for the last time at Ginger Alden's home. On August 16th 1977, "The King" Elvis Presley was found dead at his residence in Graceland.

A few hours before he died, Elvis prayed, "Dear Lord, please show me a way. I am tired and confused and I need your help." Elvis prayed this prayer in the presence of his stepbrother, Rick Stanley. Elvis also voiced to Rick a few moments before his death "Rick, we should all begin to live for Christ."

Elvis Presley Sang Gospel and Sings On

Most of Elvis' charity endeavors received no publicity at all. Throughout his adult life, for friends, for siblings, and for total strangers, he quietly paid medical bills, bought houses, supported families, paid off debts, and much more.

Elvis was a Christian and many believed that Elvis knew he was called by God to be an evangelist. In the last year of his life he sang more Gospel songs on stage, and was even known to read from the Bible on stage.

James Brown said upon the news of Elvis' death, "I wasn't just a fan, I was his brother. He said I was good and I said he was good; we never argued about that. Elvis was a hard worker, dedicated, and God loved him. Last time I saw him was at Graceland, we sang *Old Blind Barnabus* together, a gospel song. I love him and hope to see him in heaven. There'll never be another like that soul brother."

[End article]

I thought that was a good article summing up Elvis and gospel music. So much so that I felt it a great fit for my chapter on Elvis and gospel. That gives you more of a sense of his background in gospel music, if you didn't already know about it. Elvis was always in a spiritual state while singing any gospel song, but when he sang "How Great Thou Art," it was a surreal experience. It gave everybody in the audience chills. It was breathtaking.

Chapter 9: The Drugs and the Hit

Elvis had a problem with prescription drugs, although some don't want to believe it. Like most people who have that problem, the only thing that works is to stop doing it, completely. If you have had anybody in your life that had this problem, you totally understand what it is like to deal with. It's a complete nightmare, and I wouldn't wish it on my worst enemy.

One time we were in Vail, Colorado at a ski resort. I was in Elvis's room and he said, "Hey Dave, watch this." He picked up a handful of pills and swallowed them all without water. It was 16 pills; he was quite proud of that. Then he said, "Hold your hand out." I held out my hand and he dumped 16 pills in it and insisted that I take them. I told him I most certainly would not take them. "It's all right. Go ahead," he insisted.

"No, Elvis, I'm not taking them." I could see I wasn't getting anywhere with him as he just stared blankly. I saw in his eyes he wasn't giving up. "All right, I'll do it later, okay?"

"Oh, okay," Elvis replied.

I walked away irritated. I went and found Dr. Nick, Dr. George C. Nichopoulos, Elvis' personal physician. I showed him the pills and asked him what they were. He looked at the pills and asked, "Where did you get those?"

"Where do you think I got them?" I replied. "I got them from Elvis." I told Dr. Nick that Elvis insisted that I take them, but I refused.

"Good thing you didn't take them. If you had, you'd be dead right now. There would be nothing I could do to save you."

It was hard to believe how many pills Elvis took during the time I worked for him. He relied heavily on them. It seemed he took a pill for everything. He took pills to stay awake, and he took pills to go to sleep. He took pills to relax, and he took pills for energy. He popped them like Tic-Tacs. Even so, he adamantly maintained that he didn't have a problem. In addition to uppers and downers, he also took painkillers. It was so bad his system couldn't function without the drugs. He was no longer a normal human being, but a drug-ridden addict. It was hard watching him commit slow suicide.

I used to believe drugs were directly responsible for Elvis's death. I believed he woke up in the night and, not realizing he had just taken his latest dose, went ahead and took another. Since I was not there at the time of his passing, I formed my opinion based on conversations I had with a couple of the guys who were. Since those days I have changed my opinion, and now believe drugs were not the immediate cause of his death. Rather, I believe drugs wrecked his body so badly that he was susceptible to the violent heart episode that killed him.

There were several drugs in Elvis's body when he passed away. There are many conflicting stories on the Internet, and many fans want to believe the stories that attempt to prove drugs had nothing to do with his death, and that he wasn't addicted. I understand it's difficult for fans to believe their beloved star, the man they worshipped, had a drug problem. However, Elvis had 11 drugs in his system when he died—way more than any human being should have. None of the drugs, however, were illegal. He even had codeine, which he got from his dentist—unbeknownst to Dr. Nick—in his system.

As you know, I was not employed by Elvis when he died. I heard about Elvis's death when driving my car on the freeway in Southern California. I was bringing my wife a birthday present. I was listening to the radio when it was announced that Elvis Presley had died. I thought it was a mistake, so I pulled over to the side of the road to listen. It was a big story, of course, and it sunk in. It was true. Elvis was dead.

I sat at the side of the freeway in a state of disbelief. Although I wasn't a part of his life anymore, something inside me hoped I'd get a call from him to patch things up completely. I would have loved to be back in his inner circle. Even though, when I was fired, and I didn't like the way that was handled, I still loved Elvis, and deep down, I know he still loved me. I didn't want to work for him anymore, but I would have loved to hang out with him again.

Sitting in my vehicle at that moment, I felt numb. I had flashbacks of hearing Elvis's laugh. I felt as if I could still hear his voice, and in that daze, it was as if he was in the car with me. I couldn't wrap my head around the fact that I would never get to see him or hear him again. It was a horrifying feeling. I just felt helpless and empty.

By the time I got home, my phone was ringing off the hook, which was kind of interesting because it wasn't listed in my name. The media all had it, though, every one of them. One of them sent a limousine to pick me up so I could be interviewed on a TV show. I refused to do that. I refused all the other offers as well, except one. The only interview I decided to do was with Sonny the day after Elvis died.

Sonny and I did a press interview, which we knew would be difficult because of the book we had contributed to, *Elvis; What Happened?*, which had already been released. There were over 50 reporters there ready to tear our heads off. They were hostile; I mean they were *nasty*. They thought we were stupid ex-bodyguards trying to make a buck promoting the book. Their questions came at us like a barrage of bullets. The last question the reporter asked was, "If you loved him so much, why couldn't you protect him?"

I quickly responded, "Of course I loved him! How do you protect a man from himself?" That was the end of the news conference. That comment has become famous. I hear it all the time. It doesn't matter how much you love somebody, you cannot protect them from themselves.

I ended up testifying at Dr. Nick's trial; it was my testimony that got him off. Dr. Nick was not the bad guy. There *were* bad guys, but Dr. Nick was not one of them. He was the only doctor who really tried to help Elvis. I know that for a fact. After the trial, when Dr. Nick was acquitted, I was talking to the press. One of the reporters asked, "Was Elvis really a drug addict?"

"Are you fucking stupid?" I replied, right in front of everybody, including the cameras. "Listen to me," I continued. "Fact—the autopsy on Elvis's body showed that at the time of his death he had eleven different drugs in his system. If that's not an addict, I don't know what is." Some of the people who were still around Elvis when he died said he was in good health and looking forward to the next tour; he was excited about going on the road again.

There were other people who were still around Elvis when he died said, "Elvis had this disease that no one knew about." No one knew about it? Then how the hell do *you* know about it? In either case, if Elvis was in good health, why did he need to have 11 different drugs in his system? If Elvis had a disease, name the damn disease that requires the simultaneous ingestion of 11 different drugs!

Now, I'm not a doctor, but in my opinion, if drugs weren't the cause of Elvis's death, they were a contributing factor.

Some people said Elvis took drugs because he had glaucoma. Others would say he took drugs because he had bone cancer. What a crock of lying shit. None of that is true. Drugs took a decent human being, turned him into a caricature of himself—a zombie—and contributed to killing him. Every negative thing that I can think of having to do with Elvis was because of the drugs.

Elvis Presley was the greatest guy I ever met in my life. We had so much fun. He was down to earth, fun to be with, cracked jokes, laughed, and just had a wonderful time. Drugs destroyed all that. When Elvis died the world lost the greatest entertainer who ever lived. Those of us known as "The Memphis Mafia," the people who were around him, we lost somebody we considered family.

Drugs take perfectly decent and worthwhile human beings and put them in an irrational mindset where they react to life situations by acting out in bizarre ways. For family and friends, who love and care for these addicted individuals, it is a seemingly endless cycle of agony and frustration because drug addicts do not suffer alone. Their families and friends who love them suffer too. Sometimes people forget that addicts are not bad people—they're victims.

When Priscilla left Elvis for karate pioneer Mike Stone, Elvis went nuts. It was something crazy. Full disclosure: Mike Stone was a good friend of mine and still is to this day. We've been friends for over 50 years. Ever since the day I met him at Ed Parker's Studio in Pasadena, CA, we've been buddies. The day we met, we had a sparring match. He kicked my ass up and down the studio floor. I never laid a glove on him, except to give him a handshake and a hug after the match. I hope I won't cause Mike any discomfort by telling this story.

Elvis' behavior with respect to Mike Stone was pretty bizarre. You can read more about it in the book, *Elvis: What Happened?* Elvis didn't approach just Red and Sonny about having Mike Stone killed, he contacted me as well.

Elvis was somehow convinced that I had killed a few guys in a bar. I don't know where he heard such a thing. No matter how much I denied this outrageous and false story, he believed it. He'd say things like, "Tell me about that, Dave," and, "Come on, Dave, you can tell me."

In fact, the more I denied that crazy story, the more he believed it. At the end of our conversation, Elvis calmly asked if I knew some "bad guys" who would be willing to kill someone for money. I knew where he was going with this but didn't want a confrontation with him. I just said that I did know some "bad guys," but that I didn't specifically know someone who did that kind of thing.

Elvis pushed a little more and asked me if I would do some investigating. I told him I would ask around, thinking I would just blow it off and, eventually, he would come to his senses and drop it.

A few weeks went by and I thought maybe Elvis had let it go, but he hadn't. He asked me to give him a status report on my efforts to secure a hitman. For a few seconds, I didn't know what to say. Then I said, "Well, Elvis, he wants $50,000."

"Pay him," Elvis replied.

I was stunned. I didn't know what to say or do. I just stalled, once again, for a few weeks, until Elvis brought it up again. I said, "I didn't want to tell the guy, but he knows I work for you, so he upped his price to $100,000.

"Pay him," Elvis said.

At that point, I'd finally had enough. I asked Elvis if he and I could have a private conversation about it. In private, I told him, "Elvis, this is just crazy. He'll do the deed and then blackmail you the rest of your life." I made that up. I was pretty sure he had not really thought through the ramifications of such an action. "Secondly," I continued. "Mike Stone is not the bad guy here! You are!" He jerked back and looked at me, confused. "Look at the situation, Elvis. You've been screwing every chick on the planet for a long time. Do you really think your wife didn't know you were cheating on her? Of course, she did, and frankly, there is no wife that I know of who would put up with that kind of betrayal for very long without doing something about it. You embarrassed her in public for a long time. I'm amazed she took it for as long as she did. You need to drop this insane thing, Elvis. No good can come from it."

"I know. You're right Dave," Elvis replied, and that was the end of it, as far as my involvement was concerned. That was one of the most difficult situations I have ever dealt with in my life. I had never had anybody come up to me to try to get another human being killed. I had dealt with people overreacting to situations, saying stuff like, "I'm going to kill him," or, "I hope somebody shoots that guy," but then, ten minutes later, everything was fine. They were just angry and said some dumb things they shouldn't have.

This situation with Elvis was different by a long shot. When I looked into his eyes, a stranger was staring back at me: somebody evil. It was not the Elvis I once knew. He wanted Mike Stone killed, and he couldn't have been more serious. At that moment, he would have done anything to have it taken care of. It was like he went nuts and belonged in an insane asylum isolated in a padded room.

Chapter 10: Getting Fired! *Elvis What Happened?*

Elvis meant the world to me. Not because of his fame, but because of the man I knew as Elvis, the person. I loved Elvis, the person. After all these years, I'm still not sure why I was fired, but I have contemplated some possible scenarios. I don't think there is a single answer to that question even though there have been many theories brought forth regarding why I was fired, along with Red and Sonny. In my case, all the other guys couldn't figure out what I had done to deserve it. At the time, neither could I. Now I've had some time to think about the possible reasons, and I think it was a combination of things.

One of the strongest theories was that we—Red and Sonny and I—were advocating against the drugs. Most of the other guys just ignored it and were enablers. Think about that for a moment. Everyone who worked for Elvis, everyone at the various venues where we appeared, every single doctor or nurse who saw Elvis and everyone who was related to Elvis (especially his father Vernon, who paid the bills for all the drugs) knew that Elvis had a massive drug problem. Everybody was aware, but only three of us stood up to try to do something about it, and we got fired.

I think Elvis figured out that he couldn't control the three of us like he could control everybody else in his life. He was the great Elvis Presley. I think once he realized that Red, Sonny, and I were the only three people in his life he couldn't govern, he had to get rid of us. I heard later that Elvis was just trying to teach us a lesson, showing us he was still the "boss," and he planned to hire us back.

Another factor is that *nobody* said no to Elvis Presley. He was above the law. It was his way or the highway, and that's all there was to it. There was no compromise whatsoever. If you didn't agree with him, you were gone, period. As kind hearted and loving as he was, he was stubborn as a mule, especially with all the drugs in his system.

Elvis absolutely refused to believe he had a drug problem, and nobody could convince him otherwise. He believed that because he got his drugs from doctors, and that they were "legal," it must be okay to take them. Red, Sonny, and I tried to do what we could because it killed us to see him slowly killing himself. We threatened some of the suppliers to tell them we wanted them to stop. We also tried to get Elvis hooked up with a rehab facility, so he could get treatment.

It would've been a quiet process. Nobody would've known about it. We believed Elvis needed professional help. His reaction to our interceding with some of the suppliers was to tell us to leave the suppliers alone; he "needed" the drugs. His reaction to the rehab suggestion was to go berserk. He didn't believe such nonsense. When the plan was presented to him he was mortally offended, threw a monumental temper tantrum, and ordered us to leave town immediately. We left so fast that a couple of guys who stayed behind had to pack our bags for us.

People have their own theories about why we were fired, some of which are probably somewhat true, but most are just nonsense—secondhand information—speculation. If you weren't there, and you didn't know Elvis personally, you don't know what happened. Ninety-five percent or more of Elvis's fans didn't know him personally and weren't there.

The way Red, Sonny, and I were fired was particularly galling to us. Red was with Elvis since high school, Sonny was with him for 16 years or so, and I'd been with him for four. Four years doesn't seem like much, comparatively, but a lot of things happened throughout those four years. I developed a wonderful friendship with Elvis. We all had a great relationship with him. I spent many hours conversing with him about a variety of topics; I saved his ass many times; and I was his martial arts instructor. Were we suddenly incompetent to do our jobs?

In my case, the day I was fired, I went to Graceland that morning, only to notice that nobody was there. Elvis and the guys were gone, which was odd.

What was going on? I immediately received a call from Vernon asking me to come over to the office. "I want to speak to you." I went to the office and Vernon said, "We need to cut back on expenses, so we have to let you and Red and Sonny go." It was a total crock.

We knew Vernon was lying about the reason we were getting fired. I mean, come on! It was Elvis Presley! The guy spent hundreds of thousands of dollars on gifts alone, and some of those gifts were for random strangers. He didn't need to cut back on expenses. He had plenty of money.

There it was, however. I was fired, and Elvis didn't even do it in person. He left town in the dead of the night and had his father do it. To say I was pissed off would be putting it lightly. I felt I deserved respect and to be treated like a man. Elvis hired me like a man, now I felt that he needed to fire me like a man. Instead, he snuck away in the middle of the night to have somebody else do it for him. My blood was boiling worse than it ever had before.

Not firing me in person was cowardly and unacceptable. Furthermore, I was fired with three days' notice and one week's pay. That's just cold, low, and, most of all, hurtful. After everything I had done for Elvis, I just couldn't believe it. That was something I never saw coming, and because of that, I wasn't prepared for it. Several thoughts sprinted through my head, especially regarding finances. I just went from making good money to being unemployed. As much as it hurt me, I did forgive Elvis, and hoped that everything would turn out all right. Unfortunately, it didn't, and I never saw him again.

Elvis: What Happened? turned out be one of the most controversial books in the history of America. Many people have the wrong idea as to why we agreed to contribute to the book, however. I have a few reasons why I was a part of the project, and I hope to provide clarity to those who have the wrong impression. The book is still in print; you can read it for yourself.

I was a part of a show in Sweden a few years back and, afterward, spent some time with fans while drinking some wine. One of the fans said to me, "You know, Dave, the fans think that you, Red, and Sonny wrote the book just for money."

"Really," I said.

"Yeah, some people think that."

For me, there were three reasons I agreed to do the book, and money was only one of them. I already knew what many Elvis fans thought of us for writing that book. This guy was respectful and honestly wanted to know my intentions with the book. I just wish other fans would be as open and understanding as this fan was.

Regarding writing the book for the money, you must understand I was fired with three days' notice and one week's pay ($350 a week, minus all the taxes). Suddenly, I was out of a job, a 38-year-old ex-bodyguard, with no immediate prospects. What was I supposed to do? How was I going to take care of my family? So yeah, I had an opportunity to make some money, and I went with it. Don't you take some money when you work?

Over the years I have received numerous nasty statements from more than a few so-called Elvis fans. The comments are usually in the form of screaming at me for making all those millions of dollars off the book. I wish that were true, but the plain reality is that in the beginning I made 1.6¢ off each book that was sold. The book was in print for some 22 years, and over all that time I made a total of $42,000. Interestingly, we were never paid a single penny over the last 10 years the book was in print. If you think we made millions off the book, you couldn't be farther from the truth. Not even close.

Yes, I did make some money from the book and that was my first reason for agreeing to do the project. My second reason was the manner of our firing. I was totally upset that Elvis didn't respect me enough to fire me in person. It just didn't sit well with me.

Right after I was fired, I called my wife to tell her what happened. She was as shocked as I. "Elvis left town and let his father do it?" she asked angrily. "You go track him down and speak with him in person," she demanded. That's exactly what I wanted to do. I was so upset and I wanted closure.

I found out that Elvis was staying at Dr. Elias Ghanem's home in Las Vegas, so I went there the following day. He was a doctor to many celebrities. I borrowed a car from the security guys at MGM and drove out to the gated community where the doctor lived. I got through security at the gate and walked into the house wearing a gun (I was licensed to carry in Nevada). It scared the hell out of everyone in the house.

"I'm not here to hurt anyone or cause any trouble," I said to the few people in the living room. "All I want is for Elvis to face me like a man and tell me that he's firing me. He hired me to my face and he can fire me to my face. I don't want my job back, and I won't take it if he offers it to me. Where is he?"

The guys settled down and said that Elvis was upstairs in bed sleeping, under heavy sedation. That was the good doctor's weight control plan—keep the patient asleep long enough (more like being in a coma), and eventually, the patient would lose weight. He couldn't eat if he was asleep. I waited an hour to see if Elvis was going to wake up. That was an interesting hour. You could cut the tension in the room with a switchblade. I was calm as could be, however. I just wanted to say my piece to Elvis. The doctor arrived. When he saw me, he looked like he was going to have a heart attack. He quickly calmed himself when I explained to him the same thing I said to the other guys.

"Dave, he's not going to face you, but I'll tell him what you said," the doctor explained. Of course, I knew he wouldn't say anything to Elvis, but I had made my point, and left. I was hoping I would get a chance to face Elvis again at some point, just to get an understanding right from the horse's mouth. Unfortunately, it never happened.

The third reason I was willing to be a part of *Elvis: What Happened?* was that I, along with Red and Sonny, really did want Elvis to wake up and realize what he was doing to himself and everyone around him. We'd tried the best we knew how, over and over, while we were working for him because we loved him so much. We got fired for our efforts. We still wanted to see if we could do something that would motivate him to seek help and stop the train wreck he was heading for.

Immediately after we were fired, we received several offers from book publishers. We accepted an offer, and the book *Elvis: What Happened?* was produced. Sadly, once again, we failed in our efforts to get Elvis to realize he had a problem. At least we tried. We tried even with the sure knowledge that by going public with the truth we were going to catch a whole bunch of nastiness. Boy did we!

To give you a small idea, after the book came out (approximately two weeks before Elvis died), the publishers received a bunch of mail. As I understand, publishers usually receive one letter per every 700 readers. The publishers called me up. "We've got all this mail. Do you want it?"

"How much mail are you talking about?" I asked.

"Forty thousand letters."

"What do they say?"

"It's all hate mail."

"What makes you think I would like to read 40,000 hate letters calling me every vile name in the world?" I asked. I declined to view any of them.

I already felt bad enough about the immediate aftermath of the publication of that book. In retrospect, we should have collected that hate mail and saved it for the archives. It would have served as an interesting insight into fan psychology. Ah well, hindsight is 20/20.

What many of Elvis's fans don't know is that Red, Sonny, and I had no say about what got printed in the book. We were interviewed regarding various topics and situations, and the Australian tabloid journalist who wrote the book, along with those in the publishing company, had their own agendas, about which we knew nothing. They put a lot of negative stuff in that book to make it controversial and sensational thereby guaranteeing more sales.

That was not the way we thought the book would turn out. Our intentions were only to help Elvis see his problem and get help. Unfortunately, we were exploited in the process. It was pure tabloid sensationalism, and it happened without our knowledge or permission. We had spent an entire month in a hotel room answering question after question as the writer interviewed us. At least half of the information we gave him never went in the book.

I was under the impression that the book would be a more balanced presentation of Elvis, rather than focusing on his many foibles. It was infuriating when I first read it. I was upset that our input regarding what was published was ignored. Just look at what was written on the back of the book. Those words did not come out of any of our mouths. The Australian tabloid journalist or the publisher made all of it up.

Some people who were working for Elvis at the time accused Red, Sonny, and me of betraying Elvis with the book. They spouted that we stabbed him in the back, and other nasty accusations. Many fans picked up on this talk and, because it came from some folks who worked for Elvis, the fans believed it and spread it around.

Those same Elvis guys who spread the hate initially are still saying things like, "The book killed Elvis." What, seriously? Are you crazy? Are you stupid? Are you crazy *and* stupid? To those guys, I say that you should be careful about what you say about me because if you piss me off, I'll write a book about *you*, and then *you'll* die! It's stupid, but they tell those fallacies to the fans and, sadly, many of them believe it.

Over the years, I have learned not to get upset with hateful comments, but how do you think my daughters feel when they hear this garbage? How would you feel if someone viciously attacked your children in the same manner?

You see, everyone seems to be so concerned about Elvis's feelings, but hardly anyone seems to be concerned about anybody else's. It's almost like, to these folks, no one but Elvis had feelings. The reality is that *everyone* has feelings and those feelings count.

The bottom line is that those people weren't there, and I was. I hope the fans understand that most of my time with Elvis was special, and I count myself fortunate to have been a part of his inner circle. That doesn't mean everything was roses and candy. We traveled a few difficult roads while I was protecting him. That's life, folks.

When the book *Elvis: What Happened?* came out, my daughters were 10 and 12 years old. At school a girl came up to my daughter, Lori, and said, "Oh yeah, your dad is a liar. He said all these things about Elvis. He's a liar." Lori punched her out. She punched the girl in the face and knocked her out cold. The next thing you know, Lori was in the principal's office.

"You know what, young lady?" the principal said. "Your father is going to hell, and you're not far behind him." When my daughter got home that day she didn't want to tell me what had happened, but finally spilled the beans.

It's one thing if I say something. I'm a grown man, and I stand up for whatever comes out of my mouth. I said it and I'm responsible for that. If you don't like it, you can certainly come and discuss it with me, but you don't dare go to my innocent 12-year old and blast your hatred of me onto her. She had nothing to do with it.

Frankly, there were many people who were angry with me, Red, and Sonny, and thought it was perfectly fine to make my 10 and 12-year-old daughters targets for their hatred. Not on my watch.

Chapter 11: The Aftermath

When Elvis died, the world stopped. My world collapsed. Just because I was fired and hadn't spoken to Elvis in a year doesn't mean I didn't still love him. When I heard that horrific news over the car radio, I had to pull over because my tears were clouding my vision. It was horrible. All I could think about was how I wished Elvis had listened to us and gotten help with his drug problem.

It took a long time for the misery to pass by. Although nobody ever forgot about Elvis, eventually, the mourning passed and turned into celebrating his life. To this day, Elvis's spirit is alive and well. He will never die. He is still the greatest entertainer who ever lived, in my opinion. He's more famous now than when he was alive. That shows the kind of impact Elvis had on people throughout his short life.

After Elvis passed away, I ended up doing several things for work, although none were as great as being his bodyguard. I worked in real estate at Mission Hills Reality in San Juan Capistrano, CA, for a year or so. It wasn't something I wanted to make a career out of, so I moved on. For five years, I was a part of a Security Operations Group in Huntington Beach, CA, as a lecturer and training officer for police and security professionals. It included counter-terrorism, defensive driving, instinctive shooting, and unarmed self-defense.

I moved to Nevada to be a casino dealer. Over the next several years I worked in a handful of casinos throughout Nevada. Of course, my main passion and profession has always been martial arts. Throughout the years, after Elvis's death, I taught regular martial arts classes and traveled all over the world to teach Kenpo seminars.

The martial arts have defined my life; I've been a martial artist almost my entire life and made my way into the history books of Kenpo. I feel that martial art training is one of the best things one can do for oneself . . . child or adult. The benefits are endless for both adults and children—focus, respect, self-discipline, self-control, motivation, determination, goal-setting and achieving, fitness (primarily functional fitness), balance, coordination, agility, flexibility, speed, power, and self-defense, to name a few.

Aside from those just mentioned, and more, there is one benefit that I try to highlight the most—self-confidence. I feel self-confidence—the acquired ability to stand up on one's own two feet and persevere in the face of adversity— is the best benefit from martial arts training. I certainly have no quarrel with team sports and group activities; we all need to learn how to work with and interact with others. However, where's the team when you're out looking for a job? Where's the team when you're looking for a girlfriend or boyfriend? Where's the team if, God forbid, you must defend your life or somebody else's?

There is you and only you. You must be the instrument of your own salvation. Superman is not going to fly in through the window to save you. You must learn to be your own bodyguard. My experience over the years has shown me that the average kid or the average adult is quite capable of developing the skills necessary to deal with adversity of all types. Average means *you*. The self-confidence a student—child or adult—develops through small incremental successes when training in martial arts is priceless.

As an instructor, it's an amazing transformation to watch a student acquire this self-confidence. You can be sure that this skill will manifest itself in every facet of this person's life in positive ways. Suddenly, this student will not be afraid to raise their hand in history class when the teacher asks a question and the student thinks they have the answer but isn't sure, when before they would be afraid to be wrong and not raise their hand; now when a local bully makes fun of them the student won't be afraid to stand up to the bully and tell them to knock it off; and the speech they give in science class in front of classmates is something they will look forward to rather than something they are completely dreading; and most importantly, when someone tells then they are not good enough or smart enough, they finally will have the confidence to ignore them and continue to face life challenges head on succeeding in whatever they desire.

Over the course of my life, there have been and continue to be a never-ending series of "life lessons" coming my way. It seems like every time I turn around there's a new one biting me on the rear end to get my attention and tell me, "Okay, Dave, deal with this shit."

I don't know about you, but occasionally, I just get plain sick and tired of having to deal with "life lessons" all the time. Give me a break. Cut me some slack. Leave me alone for a minute. Hey, I know, let's go have a beer, kick back, and tell some lies to each other, okay?

In a more serious vein, I guess one of the most valuable lessons that I have learned is that I'm responsible for everything that has happened in my life. The consequences of my choices, whether good or bad, are mine—I own them, and they are mine to do with as I choose.

Like you and everybody else, dreadful things have happened to me in the past, and some of it was surely not my fault. Even though it wasn't my fault, how I feel and act about that stuff *is* up to me. The quote from Charles R. Swindoll says it all: "Life is about ten percent what happens to you and 90 percent how you react to it." If someone offends me in some manner, I have at my disposal any number of responses. However, regardless of how I choose to respond, the action I take is my creation. I'm responsible for that action and the consequences of that action.

In the martial arts world, I can choose to do the work necessary to achieve a black belt, win a competition, become a better person, and so on, or I can choose to not do the work and therefore never achieve anything—wasting my time and my instructor's. Either way the choice is mine or so are the rewards or consequences. It's been quite the journey. I will never forget the times I had with Elvis.

Until we meet again, boss, keep singing for the angels. I look forward to singing with you in heaven. I've heard that there is nothing negative there—so I will finally have the voice of an angel. ***TCB.***

www.ingramcontent.com/pod-product-compliance
Lightning Source LLC
Chambersburg PA
CBHW070932160426
43193CB00011B/1671